THE
CONTAINER
GARDEN

Nigel Colborn

THE
CONTAINER
GARDEN

Photographs by Marijke Heuff

Crescent Books

New York · Avenel

First published in 1990 by
Conran Octopus Limited
37 Shelton Street
London WC2H 9HN

This 1995 edition published by Crescent Books,
distributed by Random House Value Publishing, Inc.,
40 Engelhard Avenue, Avenel, New Jersey 07001.

Random House
New York ● Toronto ● London ● Sydney ● Auckland

Library of Congress Cataloging-in-Publication Data

Colborn, Nigel.
The container garden / Nigel Colborn.
p.   cm.
Originally published: London : Conran Octopus Limited,
1990.
Includes index.
ISBN 0-517-12114-X (hc) : $15.99
1. Container gardening.   I. Title.
[SB418.C64   1995]
635.9'86—dc20   94-28034
CIP

Printed and bound in Hong Kong

page 1
This bluish-mauve group uses summer plants:
lobelias, petunias and verbena.

page 2
Convolvulus mauritanicus, a blue trailing
tender perennial, flowers all summer.

page 3
A well-planned group includes euphorbia, viburnum,
pots of ivy and the early tulip 'White Emperor'.

CONTENTS

Introduction 7

THE PRINCIPLES OF CONTAINER PLANTING 9

Designing the Plan 10
Planting for Color 16
Planting for Aspect 22

CHOOSING THE CONTAINER 29

Pots and Tubs 30
Window Boxes 36
Hanging Baskets 40
Troughs and Sinks 44
Balcony Boxes 50
Raised Beds 52
Outlandish Containers 54

THE CONTAINED GARDEN 57

Using Containers 58
Balcony Gardens 62
Roof Gardens 64
Terraces and Front Gardens 74
Steps 76
Vertical Gardening 78
Container Crops 82

CONTAINERS IN THE GARDEN 89

Making the Most of Containers 90
Solving Special Problems 102
Bonsai 108
Conservatories 110
Seasonal Effects 114

GARDENING TECHNIQUES 119

The Container 120
The Soil 122
Watering and Drainage 124
Planting 126
Feeding 128
Training and Pruning 130
Propagation 134
Overwintering 137
Pests, Diseases and Disorders 138

DIRECTORY OF USEFUL PLANTS 141

Trees and Shrubs 143
Climbers and Trailers 147
Herbaceous Perennials and Alpines 150
Annuals 155
Bulbs, Corms and Tubers 156

Index 158
Acknowledgments 160

INTRODUCTION

*P*lants have been grown in containers for thousands of years. In 1500 B.C., Queen Hatshepsut of Egypt laid out a temple garden on bare rock and then filled containers with the rich alluvial silt of the Nile so that exotic plants could flourish in this inhospitable environment. Over the centuries, the idea of container gardening spread from ancient Egypt to Greece, Rome and via the Renaissance, to the modern world. Today, containers have so many uses that gardening without them seems unthinkable, and imagine how dull our communities would look without any.

Containers open up whole new worlds. Clearly, they can provide a means of gardening where cultivation might not otherwise be possible, turning barren areas into refreshing, leafy environments. But even if room is unlimited and the soil perfect, a garden without containers lacks an essential element. They enable changes to be brought about quickly by replanting, by repositioning, or even by bringing a new batch in and throwing the old out. In cold climates, tender plants can be put outdoors for summer but overwintered inside. Urns or pots can be filled with specialist composts, enabling plants which dislike local soil to thrive in the area. Culinary plants can be made to look attractive in containers while supplying food for the kitchen. In short, container gardening, far from being a single technique, embraces all aspects of conventional growing, and adds a great deal more besides.

When we moved into our present home, a horrible expanse of bare concrete adjoined the back of the house. There was neither time nor money, in that first summer, to redesign the landscape, but, with a couple of stone sinks and a number of large pots, the site was instantly transformed to a fragrant, colorful garden. We liked it so much that even though it was eventually re-paved, the containers remain there to this day, providing color and greenery throughout the year.

LEFT *Containers that have seasoned with growths of lichens make attractive features.*

THE PRINCIPLES OF CONTAINER PLANTING

Containers make it possible to grow plants where other kinds of gardening are not feasible. Additionally, with some knowledge of basic principles and a little thought and planning, they can be used to create visual and sensual interest throughout the year in virtually any situation.

Imagine, for instance, a bare terrace outside a house frontage. In your mind's eye, place a large antique lead tank there, decorated with dolphins or swans, and planted with cream tulips or fragrant wallflowers. Now think of that same site in high summer. The silver-gray leaves of *Helichrysum petiolare* cascade over the sides of the tank, making a bright contrast to the somber, crusty metal, and soft pink pelargoniums (colloquially known as pot geraniums), or deep purple heliotropes, their rich scent wafting in through the open windows of the house, blend with the silver foliage.

In this section, I discuss the principles of design, color and aspect underlying successful container gardening. These principles apply equally to roof gardens, narrow passageways, the side of buildings or even basement steps whether the containers are tubs, hanging baskets or raised beds.

LEFT Phlox *"Chattahoochee"* is superb grown on its own in a sink or trough. Its pale color will stand out clearly against a somber background of evergreens.

DESIGNING THE PLAN

The principles of good garden design apply as much to pots and boxes as they do to rolling acres. So, it is worth taking time to consider some of the basic attitudes which separate a mediocre garden from one which is a source of delight to the body and refreshment to the soul. That may sound a little over the top but, after all, Paradise is usually portrayed as a garden, and the story of Adam and Eve would not have had half so much impact if they had been expelled from, say, the Condominium of Eden! The task of every good gardener is to make her, or his, patch of soil into an earthly paradise. Here's how to do it.

KNOW YOUR STYLE

At the risk of generalizing, it is fair to say that gardening styles can be divided into two broad categories: formal or informal.

Formal designs use rigid structures and strict geometrical layouts. The "hard" landscaping features, such as walls, steps, arches and arbors, tend to be symmetrical and are often classical in design, and the "soft" landscaping is often hard-edged too, with severely clipped hedges, repetitious planting and restrictions of color.

Informal designs may still use rigid structures, but as often as not there will be some dependence on sweeping curves, and steps or walls will usually have plants growing all over them in a seemingly haphazard way.

The overall appearance, and purpose, of a well-planted formal garden is of order and symmetry, whereas an informal garden looks natural, like a piece of wild countryside. Both styles, when well-executed, are immensely attractive and pleasing, and it would be quite wrong to judge whether one has more merit

ABOVE *Evergreens, clipped into formal shapes, make good "doorkeepers."*

LEFT *Containers planted for shape and color transform an awkward corner.*

OPPOSITE *Potted hostas and hydrangeas are arranged to enhance the garden furniture.*

than the other. It is a matter for personal preference. In reality most people design gardens which exhibit a mixture of both styles, and there is nothing at all "wrong" with that. The important thing is to know which effect you are aiming for at any particular site.

GET THE BALANCE RIGHT

Garden designers are often overgenerous with their architectural features. Arches, steps, walls, raised beds, terraces and arbors can all be used to give a unifying form to a space, but sometimes they overwhelm the design and interfere with the most important part of the garden – the plants. It is the wealth of *living* material that makes a garden restful and welcoming rather than statuary or balustrading. Containers play an important role here because they can be used for structural purposes, and, at the same time, provide extra planting opportunities.

As for the plants themselves, in a well-planned garden every one of them is part of the overall structure. Trees and shrubs are especially important because they form the "skeleton" – to be fleshed out with herbaceous plants. This means that they must have shapes and sizes that will contribute to the outline of the garden, giving it solidity and height. They must also bind everything together into some sort of whole that will remain coherent throughout winter as well as summer.

PLAN FOR CONTINUITY

Anyone can put on a dazzling show in midsummer when all the bright, tender plants are in their glory. Maintaining such interest through winter requires planning.

There will be peaks and troughs. It is not possible to have every plant at its absolute best at all times. The skill lies in planting to liven up the quiet periods without diminishing the climaxes of spring and summer. The smaller the space. the more crucial good planning is.

Every plant must be evaluated in terms of what it will contribute throughout the year. What are its best months? For how long does it flower? Five weeks of spectacular color may not be worth 47 weeks of dullness. What is the foliage like? Does it make some positive contribution to the garden? With permanent plants these questions are crucial.

TOP *Climbing* Rhodochiton atrosanguineum *is used here to provide height and structure.*

ABOVE Origanum rotundifolium *and its hybrids make fine, long-lived specimen plants for containers and tolerate hot, dry conditions.*

In limited space, a tree must have good foliage all year if evergreen; if deciduous, it needs handsome fall color or attractive winter twigs. It must also make a pleasing outline which sets off other plants. Foliage is a vital element in any garden design, particularly in winter when there are few flowers. Evergreen shrubs help here, but ivies and other trailing or low-growing plants are equally important. Variegated foliage is a fine source of winter color, but must be used with care if a bilious effect is to be avoided. Winter flowers are treasures indeed, so a well-behaved winter-flowering perennial with foliage which looks good in summer is to be cherished.

In short, it is essential to plant judiciously to insure continuity of color and interest all through the year. Using containers can be enormously helpful here because it is often possible to cheat by introducing extra plants during dull periods.

REMEMBER THE BUZZ FACTOR

This has nothing to do with bees, although anything which attracts wildlife is worth considering. It is a matter of what turns you on. Whatever the fashion or the needs of your garden, it is unsatisfying to look after subjects to which you are indifferent. No plant is worth growing, especially if space is limited, unless it gives you a buzz. Aim to use only plants which delight you — by their color perhaps, or a special scent, by their rarity or even some sentimental attachment.

My wild cornflowers are smaller in size than fancy selected strains, but their azure blooms delight me because I collected the original seed from a farm in the Auvergne in central France when my children were small enough to stand in the field with wheat up to their chins. The memories flood back whenever I see the flowers: my buzz factor.

CHOOSE SUITABLE PLANTS

Grow only what likes you. This may seem obvious, but so often we struggle to get plants which are not really suited to our environment to survive. By and large, we fail or, even worse, end up with unhappy-looking specimens which spoil the rest of the show. Containers can help here because they give more control over things such as soil type, but it is still worth restricting your choice to plants which will stay healthy and perform well without too much special treatment.

THINK ABOUT ASSOCIATIONS

In haughty-cultural circles "plant association" is very much the "in" expression. All it means is grouping plants together so that they look nice. This includes the obvious rules like trying not to mask short plants with tall ones and not getting the scale wrong – planting a violet under a rhubarb, for example. There are also more subtle factors to be considered.

Blending colors so that they are restful and harmonious – or hot and jazzy, if you prefer – is a matter of artistic skill and personal choice which is easy to write about but far more difficult to put into practice. Contrasting leaf textures, shapes and sizes – lacy against broad, rough and veiny against smooth and glossy, stiff and sword-like against ferny and wavy are other aspects which need much thought, as does blending tones of leaf color to good effect.

With containers, there is an extra series of opportunities for good – and bad   association because the color, texture, shape and size of the container itself needs to be well-matched to its occupants and to their surroundings. However, containers are movable so, as your plants mature or your tastes alter, you can move them about until you achieve the combination which pleases you most.

Good results are never instantaneous, and a clever gardener will be making constant adjustments, gradually changing and improving on the planting. Gertrude Jekyll, the over-praised British garden guru of the early twentieth century, was a brilliant associator, but it took her 40 years to get the borders right in her own garden.

TOP *The tall* Nicotiana sylvestris *provides a focal point against a background of climbers.*

ABOVE *The soft yellow blooms of* Phygelius aequalis *"Yellow Trumpet" appear throughout summer, gently contrasting with its foliage.*

ABOVE *A bright grouping of summer flowers using unconventional containers is "anchored" by a small fremontodendron tree.*

ABOVE *Low plants such as this* Impatiens *can share containers with tall plants or standard shrubs, and decorate their bases.*

Besides working on associations for visual effect, it is important to consider the other senses. Smell, not only the scent of flowers but also the aromatic nature of certain species, is an important feature of a well-made garden. Some plants, such as lemon balm (*Melissa officinalis*), are worth growing for nothing more than the fresh scent of their leaves. Touch, of supreme importance to visually handicapped people, is another way to enjoy plants. Feeling the furriness of *Stachys byzantina* (syn. *S. lanata*), for example, or popping

fuchsia buds can be a delight. Even sound – the sighing of wind in a pine or the lapping of quaking aspen leaves – helps to enrich the experience of a garden.

BE REALISTIC

Every garden has its own special quirks, and every gardener is prepared to give a different level of commitment. Too many gardening books assume either that enthusiasts will abandon career and family to nurture their precious plants or that they want pretty gardens which will do absolutely everything themselves with no input at all. But a lot of people with not too much time to spare *like* weeding and seeding, and enjoy garden chores as well as the results.

As far as layout and planting are concerned, it is important, particularly when gardening in containers, to know roughly how great your commitment will be. If you spend a lot of time away, you will probably need an automatic watering system, but you should also consider growing plants which will tolerate a certain amount of neglect. If you want to spend time puttering about, practicing your gardening skills, then grow all the summer plants from seed, go in for propagation, and try raising plants which are more challenging and also more rewarding.

Knowing the limitations of the site is also essential. Day and night temperatures, prevailing wind, air currents caused by neighboring buildings, aspect and light levels all combine to provide a set of conditions special to your garden, and planting must always take this into consideration. Even if containers are your only option, planting can be used to minimize the bad effects of some of these factors and to enhance the good ones. A living windbreak, for instance, is prettier than an ill-considered fence, and the resulting shelter will enable more delicate subjects to be planted to leeward. A canopy of vines and climbers can be used not just for decoration but to provide shading for other plants below.

BELOW *This group, which includes echeverias and* Cistus *x* lusitanicus, *is ideal for a hot, dry climate where watering can be minimal.*

PLANTING FOR COLOR

It seems rather presumptuous of me to assume that I can tell you more about color than you know already. The chances are, if your home is decorated in a style you like, that you already have well-formed ideas about which colors you enjoy and which color combinations you dislike.

Garden writers, especially snobbish ones, love to lay down the law about "good taste." But what does that mean? Are bright colors in bad taste? Is it wrong to delight in garish gladioli or dazzling dahlias? Be warned: the same garden writers who make you feel un-

easy about the vulgarity of large-flowered hybrids will moan with ecstasy over a leaf with hardly distinguishable gold veining, or gaze in rapture at a nondescript weed, when a more balanced gardener would assume that the former was diseased, while simply hoeing out the latter.

Color is a matter for personal choice, and so it should remain. However, there are certain aspects of color usage which are special to gardening, and they should not be overlooked when planning a planting scheme for your container garden.

ABOVE *Cream pansies,* Veronica gentianoides *and forget-me-nots create a cool group.*

ABOVE LEFT *Hot colors used sparingly make effective highlights. These dahlias enliven a subtle assembly of green plants.*

ABOVE RIGHT *A white group,* Impatiens *and taller lantana, contrasts with dark foliage.*

RIGHT *This pink* Verbena *"Sissinghurst," in its shapely urn, makes a fine contrast with the silver-leaved artemisia.*

RIGHT Tropaeolum peregrinum *is an easily grown, climbing annual which, as well as having handsome foliage, flowers for most of the summer. Sow seed each spring.*

BELOW *A delightfully informal effect using cool colors is achieved here with a mix of* Plumbago auriculata *and fennel which has been allowed to run to seed.*

Flower size The larger the flower, the more difficult it is to site the plant without creating clashes of color.

Think of a meadow thick with wild flowers. Yellow buttercups, pink campion, blue speedwells, rusty sorrel, purple vetch, scarlet pimpernels all grow happily at random together, making a delightful overall picture, the colors blending perfectly.

Now imagine a border with a bright purple cranesbill next to scarlet poppies which grow in front of a salmon-pink rose, through which climbs plum-colored clematis. Just to complete the display, picture a huge, ocher-yellow dahlia, one of those monsters with 12-inch blooms, square in the middle, and, for good measure, put alternating orange French marigolds and blood-red salvias along the front of the border.

The colors in the garden border clash because the flowers are so large. They make big splashes of hue, whereas in the meadow the colors appear as tiny dots like a pointillist painting. Thus, the larger the flowers, the more care you need in placing them.

Number of shades The fewer the colors, the easier it is to grade and match them. Informal, cottage-style plantings usually carry a wider range of colors than formal bedding, but when too many shades from a number of different groups get mixed together, the overall effect is muddled.

Blues and yellows, for example, can be used to contrast with each other, and there are a large number of plants from which to choose. But once your selection begins to stray toward the edges of the range and into purple

LEFT *Spring bulbs make perfect container subjects. These tulips are providing a fine splash of early color, and make a delightful contrast with the forget-me-nots.*

BELOW *The solid shapes of clipped evergreens play a useful structural role in summer displays. In winter, they may offer the only interesting focus in the garden.*

or orange, even though those colors also go wonderfully together, you have changed the ground rules, and using all four colors together could simply create a mess.

Seasonal changes "Plan your garden as though you were decorating a room," say some garden experts. But who has a room which changes in shape and hue from day to day? What interior has colors which are sharp and clear on a dewy morning in late spring, but whose shading has become tired and blowsy six weeks later? Whose living-room walls and curtains are green in spring and summer, golden yellow, red and brown in fall and gray in winter? In a garden, you have to approximate with color. It's a far more fluid business than designing interiors with man-made colors – thank heavens!

Bearing these factors in mind – and the principles apply as much to containers as to any other kind of gardening – devise color schemes to suit your own personal taste. Very broadly speaking, colors can be classified as "hot" or "cool." The charts on pages 20–21 give examples of both color ranges, with plants grouped according to season and type to provide the desired effect.

Silver foliage is uniquely valuable in planting schemes because it can contrast or harmonize with almost any color. Burning reds or vibrant pinks are toned down, but with blue and cream shades the soft, cool effect is enhanced. Luckily the choice of plants with silver foliage is wide, and, though they may prefer warm, dry growing conditions, there are several, such as *Salix lanata* (woolly willow), which are shade-tolerant.

HOT COLORS
BRIGHT GOLDS, RUSTS, REDS, YELLOWS (STRIDENT, NOT LEMON) AND ORANGE

	SHRUBS	HERBACEOUS
SPRING	Azaleas: "Gibraltar" – flame orange; the Mollis Azaleas – orange, salmon red; "Nancy Waterer" – sharp yellow. Berberis: *B.* x *stenophylla* – yellow flowers; *B. thunbergii* "Atropurpurea Nana" – purple foliage. *Chaenomeles* x *superba*: "Crimson and Gold;" "Rowallane" – blood red. *Cornus alba*: "Spaethii" – yellow variegations, red stems; "Westonbirt" – green leaves, crimson twigs. *Forsythia* x *intermedia* "Lynwood" – yellow. Rhododendrons: "Elisabeth Hobbie" – blood red; "Elizabeth" – scarlet; "Gigha" – claret. *Ribes sanguineum* "Brocklebankii" – gold foliage, red flowers. *Spiraea* "Goldflame" – orange foliage.	Pansies, winter; "Universal Apricot;" "Universal Yellow" Primulas (polyanthus and modern florist's primrose) – red, orange or yellow. Trollius (Globe flower) – orange or yellow. Tulips: "Apeldoorn" – red; "Golden Harvest" yellow; "Princess Irene" – orange; "Shakespeare" – salmon red. Wallflowers – especially scarlet, orange – yellow strains
SUMMER	Any shrub with gold or bronze foliage. Bougainvilleas – orange, salmon or purple. *Buddleia* x weyeriana – salmon or orange. *Euphorbia pulcherrima* (poinsettia) – red. *Euryops pectinatus* – sharp yellow. *Hypericum* species – all yellow. Roses: "Canary Bird" – bright yellow; "Maigold" – orange; "Scarlet Fire" (Scharlachglut).	Begonias: "Nonstop" strain – red, yellow, orange, pink or white. Calendulas: many varieties, all orange or yellow. Eschscholtzias (Californian poppies) – orange, yellow, salmon or lemon. Nasturtium – red, orange, yellow. Petunias: many varieties especially "Crimson Star" – red and white; "Razzle Dazzle" – mixed and white; "Red Picotee." Tagetes (African and French marigolds) – many varieties, all orange or yellow.
FALL	Most deciduous shrubs. Cotoneasters: most species – red berries. Hollies: *Ilex aquifolium* and cultivars – red, yellow or orange berries. *Pyracantha* "Orange Glow" – orange berries; *P. atalantioides* – red berries.	Chrysanthemums – all bronze or yellow varieties. *Crocosmia*: "Emily Mackenzie" – orange; "Solfatare" – yellow, bronze foliage. *Iris foetidissima* – orange fruits. Rudbeckias: "Goldilocks" – yellow with black eye; "Marmalade" – orange; "Rustic Dwarfs" – mahogany to orange shades.

COOL COLORS
PALE BLUES, LEMONS, WHITES, DARK GREENS, OFF-WHITES TO PINK OR MAUVE, SILVER FOLIAGE, GLAUCOUS FOLIAGE

	SHRUBS	HERBACEOUS
SPRING	*Exochorda* x *macrantha* – pure white. *Myrtus communis* – evergreen with white flowers. *Pieris japonica* – evergreen, small white flowers. Rhododendrons: *R. yakushimanum* and hybrids – pink shades; *R.* "Blue Tit" – blue; *R.* "Chink" – pale yellowish green.	Crocus: blue and white varieties especially "Violet Queen," "Pickwick" – striped. Forget-me-nots – all varieties. Hyacinths: "City of Haarlem" – cream; "Delft Blue;" "L'Innocence" – white. *Lathyrus vernus* var. *cyanus* – deep blue. *Lunaria rediviva* – lilac white. *Narcissus:* "Paper White;" *N. poeticus* – white, red eye; "Jenny" – cream fading to white, reflexed petals. *Pulmonaria saccharata* – blue flowers, spotted foliage. Tulips: "Groenland" – pink and green; "Purissima;" "Spring Green" – white and green; "White Triumphator."
SUMMER	Buddleias: "Lochinch" – pale blue; "White Cloud." Ceanothus: "Blue Mound;" "Cascade" – blue. *Caryopteris* x *clandonensis* – silvery blue. *Philadelphus* "Manteau d'Hermine" – white. *Viburnum plicatum* – white.	All plants with silver foliage. *Ageratum:* many varieties – blue. *Aquilegia alpina* – blue. *Campanula isophylla* – blue or white. Geranium species: *G.* "Buxton's Blue;" *G. clarkei* "Kashmir White;" *G. pratense* – blue. *Impatiens:* many varieties. Petunias: "Resisto Blue;" "Super Cascade Lilac;" "Yellow Magic."
FALL	*Ceanothus* "Autumnal Blue." *Choisya ternata* (Mexican orange) – white flowers, second flush. *Clerodendrum trichotomum* – white flowers, blue-black berries. Conifers (blue): especially *Chamaecyparis lawsoniana* "Pembury Blue;" *Picea glauca; Chamaecyparis pisifera* "Boulevard." *Ceratostigma willmottianum* – deep blue. Holly: *Ilex aquifolium* "Silver Milkmaid" – pale variegated. Rose: "Prosperity" – lemon cream, late flowering. *Sorbus cashmiriana* – white berries. *Viburnum farreri* – white.	*Aconitum carmichaelii* (monkshood) – blue. Asters: especially *A.* x *frikartii* "Mönch" – lavender blue; *A. novi-belgii* – blue forms; *A. thomsonii* – lavender blue. Chrysanthemums – cream and white forms. *Gentiana asclepiadea* – deep blue. *Kniphofia* "Percy's Pride" – greenish yellow. *Schizostylis coccinea* "Alba" – white.

PLANTING FOR ASPECT

Planting in specific garden contexts will be covered in later chapters. But, before looking at containers within the conventional garden or at gardens composed entirely of containers, it is useful to consider the conditions in which your containers may find themselves when you have positioned them. The three examples which follow are all typical situations.

COOL, PARTIAL SHADE

This aspect is less than ideal for maximizing color, but it is probably one of the most commonplace environments in urban gardens. The problem, if shade is seen as a problem, may be an overall lack of sun or only partial sunlight, either because of deep shadow caused by high buildings or shade thrown by trees. In hot climates, shade can be a distinct advantage, but in most temperate gardens too much shade, especially when accompanied by

ABOVE *Ferns and hostas prefer a cool, shady spot but dislike drought, so they are not a good choice if regular watering will be a problem. This pair creates exciting contrasts of leaf shape, texture and color.*

OPPOSITE Hydrangea macrophylla *thrives in containers and comes in many varieties, some with lace-cap flowers, others with mopheads, like these. In some varieties, acid compost results in blue flowers.*

dry soil, does impose certain limitations on the choice of plants.

Now that *Impatiens* (Busy lizzie), which flowers freely in shade, comes in such a wide range of colors, it is easier to brighten up dark corners. It is important to remember, however, that certain shades, particularly salmons, oranges and scarlets, can almost glow in the gloom – an advantage in some eyes but not in others. Deep blues, on the other hand, which look so wonderful in sunlight, almost disappear in shade.

White is useful in shady positions, but keep two points in mind: (a) no two species are ever the same shade of white and so, planted close together, one will make the other look less white, and (b) whites are inclined to pick up colors from their neighbors. Neither of these characteristics is a disadvantage, but you need to remember them.

Planting in shade, I would gravitate to pale flowers which show their subtleties of color by day and which glow by twilight. The occasional darker color will help to accentuate the delicate tones of the rest.

For skeleton planting, ivy will trail beautifully. Varieties such as "Eva," which has sage-green and white variegations and medium-sized foliage, are especially good, but any pale-leaved form would be useful. If the site is nearly frost-free, evergreens could be represented by bays, myrtles or citrus trees – a small lemon, perhaps, or the orange, x *Citrofortunella mitis,* whose white blossom provides strong fragrance. Among the blue tones, plumbago makes a wonderfully cool, pale haze, and will climb to form a screen.

Selecting soft creams or whites among the lower flowers will continue the cool theme. *Phygelius aequalis* "Yellow Trumpet," for example, with its lemon-cream flowers, blooms constantly through the growing season, and looks pleasant with blues; it also associates well with hotter colors. For more dazzling white effects, especially if these are to be contrasted with emerald-green ferns, try planting *Impatiens* – such as "Accent White" – or white azaleas.

In colder areas, dwarf rhododendrons, such as *Rhododendron yakushimanum* or its hybrids, would provide rusty-green foliage all year, but give a short burst of spectacular flowers in spring. For height, if it is too cold for plumbago to overwinter, a screen furnished with different varieties of clematis would do well, providing a display in whatever colors you wanted, from white through blues and purples to wine red. But clematis are ugly in winter, so evergreen climbers – possibly ivy again – need to be plaited through the screen as well.

Spring could be graced with sweet violets. Double Parma violets such as "Marie Louise" (violet-blue) and "Compte Brazzi" (white) have the best scent; even their leaves smell of violets. To these could be added white hyacinths and, possibly, a few white narcissi – "Paper White" or *Narcissus poeticus* – or the huge white tulip *Tulipa fosteriana* "Purissima," sometimes known as "White Emperor." If the bulbs are planted deeply enough, they can be left in situ year after year. Ivory wallflowers, or a drift of the white-flowered variegated honesty *Lunaria annua* "Alba Variegata," would be a wonderful spring addition here, binding all that paleness together.

Summer could be a time for exciting additions of temporary color – either maintaining the coolness with, say, a brilliant white lantana or the peacock-blue *Salvia patens* – or going for a change to the pink range with *Begonia semperflorens*. Alternatively, the planting could be kept simple with white roses, underplanted with alyssum. Some pelargoniums (geraniums), though they flower more freely in sun, will bloom for long periods. The F1 hybrid "Ringo White" has superb, vibrant green foliage as well as pure white flowers, and "Hollywood Star" has rose-pink flowers paling to white at their centers.

The white and green theme can be carried further by using different species of shade-loving ferns. Besides having a wide variety of interesting leaf shapes, many of them are evergreen, and in spring the young emerging fronds have a freshness of color and an airy

ABOVE *A half barrel planted with a hosta in full flower makes a fine focal point for this corner. Though they enjoy life in containers, all hostas need cool roots.*

grace which make them the most appealing companions for flowers.

The arum-lily *Zantedeschia aethiopica*, besides having huge, white flowers, produces a constant supply of bold foliage, making it an excellent contrast for ferns. It needs moist soil with a high peat content to perform well. Hybrids with colored flowers and flecked foliage are also available.

DEEP SHADE

Sometimes, a site is so gloomy that the choice of plants is severely limited. However, there are plants which will tolerate the most Stygian

ABOVE *Even if space is restricted, going for large-leaved plants like rodgersias, ferns and even a young banana helps to create a lush, tropical effect.*

there happen to be any male hollies in the vicinity, it will bear red berries. In a tropical climate, *Ficus benjamina* can be clipped and trained exactly as bay.

Few herbaceous plants will flower well in deep shade, but bulbs which are replaced each year give a dependable show because they call on reserves of food they have stored when growing in the light in previous years. Since pale colors show best in gloom and scent is an added advantage, white narcissi or hyacinths are dependable. Lily-of-the-valley has good durable foliage, and will flower in dense, dry shade. The scent of its blossom alone makes it a contender, but there is a lot of foliage for not much bloom.

In summer, color may have to come from foliage rather than flower. The rock cress *Arabis ferdinandi-coburgii* is too small to warrant such a regal name, but has rosettes of dazzling white and green which color pinkish in hard weather and seem happy in deep shade. Some fleshy-leaved sedums will spread, but are shy to flower, unlike London pride, *Saxifraga* x *urbium*, a pretty and easy saxifrage with leathery leaves and sprays of soft pink flowers. There is a variegated form which colors up well in winter.

HOT, BRIGHT SUN

Where summer rainfall is low, days are long and hot, and the site is in full sun, the first limiting factor in the environment is usually the shortage of water. If you can be sure that the plants are never likely to run dry – either by being diligent about watering or by installing a good automatic system – the choice of what to grow is vast.

Hot, bright sun gobbles up color, so what would be loud and garish in shade may look pleasantly bright in dazzling sun. Orange dahlias, nasturtiums, French marigolds or *Tropaeolum peregrinum* all make a delicious contrast with the blue of a clear sky. In certain circumstances, sharp reds and burning oranges may even go side by side in fiery glory without clashing at all.

conditions, and their chances of survival are increased enormously if care is taken with all other aspects of their environment. They must be well-nourished, therefore, in well-designed containers, and will need to be kept disease and pest-free.

A small tree might survive in a tub, and still leave room for plants at its base. Bay, especially clipped into a shape, can be surprisingly durable and shade-resistant, but it will not tolerate deep frost. Holly is tougher – though not all species are root-hardy – and it clips well into bobbles or columns. One variety, *Ilex aquifolium* "Green Pillar," grows naturally into a column, and is female so, if

With all the potential for summer jazziness, it is easy to forget about the duller months. Skeleton planting is essential to carry the display through winter. Besides broad-leaved evergreens, you could use conifers or small trees with pleasing outlines. *Picea glauca* var. *albertiana* "Conica," for example, will stay small for years, and has gorgeous blue foliage. Planted beside the purple-leaved Japanese maple, *Acer palmatum* "Atropurpureum," the contrast is superb, but remember that the acer would take exception to extremes of heat and light.

In summer, petunias would revel in the sun, as would dwarf pelargoniums. Dark-leaved forms with strong red flowers would be good or, for trailing over the sides, "Balcon Royale" provides an endless run of scarlet flowers. The solidness of the red could be broken up with the trailer *Helichrysum petiolare*.

Something cooler, and a foil for the blue *Picea glauca*, would be *Convolvulus sabatius* (syn. *C. mauritanicus*) – a tender bindweed with elegant trailing habits and lavender-blue flowers which go on into the fall. If there is enough room, *Thunbergia alata*, a climber with tangerine flowers whose centers are navy blue, can hang well, but is rather invasive. There are pale forms, and even one, "Susie," without the dark eye – a pity because the charm of this species lies in those blue-black flower centers.

THE PROBLEM CONTAINER

Every garden has its problem area. There are a variety of reasons for failure – a windy corner perhaps, a patch of ground which is too sheltered and runs short of rain, or possibly a pocket of soil which is inadequately drained.

OPPOSITE *A problem site where there is no soil can be transformed by strategic placing of containers. Here gloomy surroundings are illuminated with antirrhinums and a small bowl of biting stonecrop* (Sedum acre).

RIGHT *The somber color of a group of disciplined evergreens is contrasted with the brilliance of the pink* Impatiens. *The old water-butt helps to balance the grouping.*

In my own garden, there is a zone which I call the Bermuda Triangle, because whatever I plant there mysteriously disappears within a few months.

One way of overcoming such a patch, especially if the problem is caused by the soil rather than by climate, is to use containers. But if conditions make even container growing difficult, all is not lost. Lowering your standards is not admitting defeat — it is merely a way of compromising with hostile elements. (Politicians do little else!)

So, even if it is not possible to grow glorious plants in that benighted spot, you may still be able to manage something that is green and alive. *Aucuba japonica*, an unfairly maligned evergreen, will grow tolerably well in the gloomiest shade, and has some handsome cultivars. The non-variegated varieties, such as "Salicifolia" or "Nana Rotundifolia," have strange, sea-green stems, and, if planted near a male such as "Lance Leaf," will produce sparkling red berries.

If the site is windy, plant robust evergreens like cherry laurel, or try some of the dwarf willows. *Salix lanata* and *S. helvetica* have pretty winter twigs, silvery summer foliage and are utterly wind-resistant, as is *S. hastata*, whose twigs are like polished ebony and contrast superbly, in spring, with its gleaming white catkins and pale green emerging leaves.

Low, mound-forming perennials are frequently too small and squat to be bothered by wind, and can survive any amount of buffeting. Little bulbs also tolerate harsh conditions, flowering as they do before winter is over.

Often the only way to find out whether something will grow is to plant it and see. You may end up with a collection of half-dead twigs, but at least you will have the satisfaction of knowing that you tried.

Extremes of drought can be difficult for plants to tolerate, but cactus species and succulents will put up with the most miserable conditions and, even if their beauty is not remarkable, at least there will be something living to enjoy in an otherwise barren spot.

In extremes of frost, losses just have to be made up when spring finally arrives. Since plants are, when you consider how much skill and expertise goes into their production, so cheap, it should not hurt to have to buy at least a few replacements each season. Where space is short and growing is limited to containers, this is even more important. Nothing spoils a planting so much as tightfistedness!

If, in spite of impeccable plantsmanship, the site still proves to be too inhospitable for anything to thrive, it may be better to admit defeat than to have a container full of languishing specimens which look as though they need to be put out of their misery. However, since plants of one kind or another will grow almost anywhere, the site that grows nothing is a rarity.

CHOOSING THE
CONTAINER

*A*nything which will hold enough soil to support a plant can be used as a container. There are many different shapes and sizes of containers made from a rich variety of materials ranging from paper to stone, from plastic to concrete. There are containers specifically designed to hold plants and others which have been adapted. I have seen any number of unconventional objects used as planters – from an old roofing tile holding barely a spoonful of soil to a fishing boat.

Each kind of container has its own peculiarities, and it is worth looking at the main types in some detail to see how the best can be got out of them. With the more specialized kinds, there is little choice – a window box is a window box – but when choosing the most suitable free-standing containers for your garden, besides considering materials and style, practical considerations such as capacity and drainage are also important. On the following pages I discuss all these points as well as make planting suggestions for different types of containers. Key factors for practical success are listed on pages 119–139.

LEFT *Whether planted or just standing empty, these distinctive containers are in perfect harmony with their fall surroundings. The difference in height, the narrow decorative ribbing on one, and even the greater effect of weathering on the left-hand jar provoke a certain quiet pleasure.*

POTS AND TUBS

This is rather a catch-all group in which I am including more or less anything freestanding. Size varies from the very small to something needing a winch to lift it. Style can be anything from the classic flowerpot shape to a sawn-off beer barrel, and the material could be as elegant as lichened terracotta or as ugly as a recycled automobile tire.

As far as plants are concerned, the larger the container, the happier they are. Room for roots is essential, but most large containers are also more pleasing to look at than very small ones, partly because they make their setting look less tiny and also because large pots allow plants to reach a bigger size and therefore make a more positive contribution. It is also difficult to house collections of different plants in a single pot unless it is roomy enough for them all to develop properly, so, if you intend to compose a mixed planting, the first requirement is to invest in containers which are big enough.

From the practical point of view, however, the bigger the pot or tub, the more difficult it is to move. Since one of the great pluses of container gardening is mobility, this could lose you quite a big advantage. But large pots, even if they weigh more than 110 pounds, can be moved on a sack barrow. Tilt the pot to slide the business end of the barrow under the base, and then tie the pot to the shafts with a cord to prevent it from toppling.

If you feel disinclined to buy a sack barrow for one 20-minute session a year, it can be borrowed, perhaps from a friendly moving man. An alternative is the kind of trolley home mechanics use to slide in and out from under their cars. If you are moving pots of mature plants, take care not to injure them, especially trailing stems, which can be crushed against the sides of the pot.

Smaller pots are easier to move. They can also be grouped more easily – either spaced formally or clustered together, so that, although each contains no more than a plant or two, the assembled mass gives a fine composite result. Such arrangements give plenty of flexibility – as plants fade or if there are

deaths, the groups can be rearranged with offending pots removed and replacements added. Variability of sizes and shapes need not detract; indeed, with careful arrangement, it can be a distinct advantage.

ABOVE *Painted a dark color, the Versailles tub grabs none of the attention.*

OPPOSITE TOP LEFT *The half tub is an inexpensive but attractive container.*

OPPOSITE TOP RIGHT *An elegant container is planted with Erigeron for lasting color.*

OPPOSITE BOTTOM LEFT *Grape hyacinths provide spring color in these old clay pots.*

OPPOSITE BOTTOM RIGHT *This earthenware pot blends well with the rather bilious petunias.*

Unless the pots are themselves especially beautiful, it is often best to arrange them so that as many as possible are concealed by the flowers and foliage of the plants they contain. Grading for size will assist here, the objective being to arrange your pots so that the foliage of plants at the back rests on the rims of the pots in front of them, and so on.

Stability is an important consideration. Pots which are narrower at their bases than at their rims are more likely to blow over, particularly if the plants have grown tall, than are straight-sided, squat affairs which may look far less elegant. Providing support can help here, but the leverage of wind on a potted shrub or tree should not be underestimated.

Styles and materials are for you to decide. You know what you like, so it is quite out of order for me to pontificate about taste, particularly when I have no idea what your garden looks like. However, I cannot resist making just a few comments.

Space-age plastic plant-holders might raise a few eyebrows if they stood outside a colonial mansion, so it makes sense, where feasible, to match the style of pot to your house and to the types of structure used in the garden. If, like me, you live in a quaint old farmhouse but can barely afford to pay the repair bills, you will not want to litter the garden with expensive – and eminently stealable – antiques. I prefer to use plain pots, and encourage the plants to conceal as much of them as possible, rather than resort to some of the appalling cheap imitations making the rounds these days.

TOP *Unconventional containers like this old pail must be provided with adequate drainage holes, or the soil will quickly become waterlogged and plants will not flourish. The pansies are short-term plants.*

ABOVE *These* Viola tricolor *have self-sown around the container with charming results. Establishing a unit between the border and a solitary container can present problems for the garden planner, but here nature has suggested one very happy solution.*

OPPOSITE *Even an old zinc bath can make a handsome container with sensitive planting. Filled here with* Exacum affine, *the mauve flowers complement the soft gray of the metal sides beautifully.*

There are good reproductions to be had, but sometimes these exceed even the antiques in price. Concrete conjures up bad images, but can be surprisingly convincing, especially when the mix contains a percentage of natural stone, and even more so when it has stood for a year or two and grown a crust of moss or lichen. The so-called "Versailles tub" – a square, timber affair with a knob at each corner and often painted white – comes in tropical hardwood (very expensive) or fiberglass (expensive) which looks as good as the real thing; the design is especially suitable for clipped, formal evergreens.

Most plastic looks nasty, but imitation Georgian urns, especially white ones, have a particularly tacky appearance and do little to enhance a planting. Plastic which looks just like terracotta has been introduced recently and, if it is able to support colonies of moss or lichens, which I doubt, and can stand year after year in sunlight without losing its color or degrading, which I also doubt, it will be a useful new material.

PLANTING

Pots are so variable and so versatile that it is pointless to try to provide anything but rough guidelines. On pages 22–27, I looked at planting for different aspects, in shade and in sun, but here the focus is on planting to suit the container.

The basic message, as far as pots and tubs are concerned, is: different plants look better in different styles of container.

I've already mentioned Versailles tubs for formally clipped evergreens, but there are other examples. The Japanese grass hakonechloa, for example, looks marvelous in a low, glazed earthenware pan. Hostas also look better in low-slung containers, whereas trailers and danglers like *Plectranthus coleoides* or *Glechoma hederacea* "Variegata" need height to be able to show off their features. Highly decorated pots would do better with a sparing use of trailing plants or none at all, so that their beauty can be fully enjoyed.

TOP *This small urn, planted with large fuchsias, will need frequent watering.*

ABOVE *Diascias (rear) and an ampelopsis (in the earthenware pot) create a pink theme.*

LEFT *Freestanding clay pots of arums can, in cold areas, be overwintered under glass.*

OPPOSITE *In an informal garden, groups of containers, in this case on a circular, slightly raised bed, create a focal point.*

WINDOW BOXES

It is possible to purchase ready-made window boxes, but, more often than not, it is far more satisfactory to have them specially constructed so that their dimensions match those of the window. If you are lucky enough to have a say in the design of the box, do bear three important points in mind.

Capacity The larger and deeper the box is, the more compost it will hold and therefore the longer it can be left without watering. Further, the plants will perform all the better for having a long, cool rootrun.

Position A large box resting on a small window ledge can rob a room of a great deal of daylight. If the upper edge of the box can be set at the same level or even a little lower than that of the window ledge, it allows more scope for exuberant plant growth, and is much easier to manage because it is more accessible from an open window – especially the sash type.

Drainage Structural problems can result if water seeps into masonry or under wooden window ledges. The box must be properly installed, with drainage holes set so that the water drips straight out onto the ground – or onto passing pedestrians – rather than standing underneath or running along the bottom. That way you have no worries, depending, of course, on who the pedestrians are!

PLANTING

Successful planting in a window box is quite an art. It looks easy until you try it. Unlike pots, window boxes are not mobile since, for reasons of safety, they need to be secured. They are also one shape – long and narrow. Visually, they offer more when viewed from the outside than from the inside. All this probably seems obvious, but it is important to remember these constraints because they prescribe the way in which the box can be planted. To make changes, the plants, rather than the container, will have to be moved, so getting the selection right is far more critical.

TOP *A window box simply planted with white azaleas and prostrate juniper looks splendid.*

ABOVE *This gaily planted window will delight those inside with the scent of sweet peas.*

TOP *The "Universal Blue" winter-flowering pansy brightens up the coldest months.*

ABOVE *Swiss chalets are incomplete without pelargoniums cascading from their balconies.*

Without erect plants, the box may look "bottom heavy," but, with anything other than dwarf shrubs or low-growing herbaceous plants, you lose your view. Where windows have drapes, taller plants on either side of the box will make a variation in the outline viewed from outside, but will not spoil the interior aspect because the drapes obscure that portion of the window anyway.

Dwarf pelargoniums (geraniums) stay low enough to provide a little interest from the inside, but most of the outside display will come from trailing plants. The universally grown *Lobelia erinus*, particularly the trailing form, is yet to be superseded for dependability and for color, particularly now that the range runs through several shades of blue, rosy pink, purple and pure white. Of ivy-leaved and pendulous pelargoniums, the "Balcon" and "Breakaway" series flower forever, but old cultivars like the subtly variegated "L'Elegante" are still widely grown and for good reason.

Pure foliage effects can be achieved with a multitude of pendulous species, of which *Helichrysum petiolare* (syn. *H. petiolatum*) is one of the most popular; it turns up in several garden forms nowadays but none so lovely as the plain silver. For year-round trailers, the ivies are unbeatable, and come in all sorts of leaf shapes and colors. The bolder the variegations, the less vigorously the plants grow: too much vigor is a distinct disadvantage as far as window boxes are concerned. There are many more interesting and unusual plants (see pages 147–149), but these make a useful hardcore of trailers and danglers.

One point about window boxes frequently overlooked is their ability to house plants which can be encouraged to climb up onto nearby walls and around the window frames. Plants which are self-clinging are easiest to manage in this context, but remember the larger the mass of living plant, the heavier the

OPPOSITE *This ground-level window box has done a little too well, obscuring the windows, but what a splendid mass of color!*

demand on the limited resources of the box. A luxuriant growth all around the window frame will need far more feed and water than a small window box can provide.

The plants you choose will depend not only on local climatic conditions but also on the aspect. A wall which never receives direct sunlight is quite different from a hot, sunny elevation. Each has its own set of problems and its own advantages. On the cool side of a building, some kinds of fern which would burn up in sun are perfectly at home in a window box. Flowering plants are harder to establish in dense shade. They may survive well enough but will be reluctant to flower. The big exception is *Impatiens*, which will even flower in deep gloom and last all summer.

From inside the house, the window box is always less exciting. The daylight tends to throw the plants into silhouette, so there is little point in trying to make the perfect show from within. Scent can be a saving grace here, and whatever the window box may contain for looks from the outside, it *must* have at least one plant which will waft flower perfume or leaf aromas into the room. Heliotrope, scented-leaved pelargoniums, mignonette *(Reseda odorata)*, and Parma violets are all examples of window-box plants which will smell delicious when the windows are open.

For a truly aromatic feast, and a useful source of culinary material as well, how about a window box planted entirely with herbs? Many herbs have colored-leaf cultivars which are as good for the kitchen as the plain green varieties. Sage, for example, comes in gold, purple or purple and white variegations as well as plain green; oregano has a fine golden-leaf form, and there are several charming thymes and lemon thymes. There are also a bright-pink-flowered chive – *Allium schoenoprasum* "Forescate" – and a gorgeous, though frost-tender prostrate rosemary with bright blue flowers called "Severn Sea."

The secret of which combination of plants does best for your conditions may only be revealed by trial and error. Be adventurous therefore, and have the courage to fail!

HANGING BASKETS

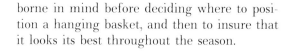

Hanging baskets can transform the otherwise drab side of a building or a dull alley, even where there is hardly any space. All you need is a hook! Cities and towns which take pride in their surroundings adorn street lamps, doorways, shopping malls, restaurants, institutional buildings and plazas with hundreds of them. But equally in either private gardens large enough for lawns and borders or where there is only room for a few containers, well-filled hanging baskets are one of the most effective ways of bringing an otherwise plantless area to life.

Though far from difficult to maintain, there are certain considerations which must be

borne in mind before deciding where to position a hanging basket, and then to insure that it looks its best throughout the season.

Watering Hanging baskets are difficult to water, and may even need special watering equipment. If the compost has been allowed to dry out, it is almost impossible to get it thoroughly moist again. If you have a number to water, a hose with a long lance attachment is essential and also far safer than the alternative – a stepladder and watering can. If there is an automatic fertilizer dispenser attached to the hose, so much the better.

Feeding Baskets are hungry. There is never a generous quantity of compost for the mass of plant material expected to grow, so a weekly feed is advisable; a biweekly one is essential. Failure to feed shortens the season, and makes for less resilient plants.

Seasonal Although winter hanging baskets are possible, especially in warm countries, the choice of plant material is far more limited than in summer, when the trailing plants already mentioned in the window-box section are at their best.

Wind Anyone who has seen a basket rocking in the wind knows that, although the plants might survive the occasional buffeting, constant wear and tear in a windy position will usually result in an ugly mess. When baskets are hung in a position regularly afflicted with a prevailing wind, they will grow lopsided with lush growth to leeward and thin, hard unproductive stems to windward.

There is no great mystery about the anatomy of a successful hanging basket. Tough wire mesh is the most common outer material. It should have gaps or openings large enough to insert plants at various levels and be stout enough not to collapse under its own mature weight. Baskets with solid sides, which allow planting only at the top, are less effective and need a higher proportion of trailing species.

The hook and fixing on which the basket depends must also be strong enough, not merely to take the dead weight of a full, wet basket but to withstand wind rocking, children having fun, cats leaping on board and so on.

Within the wire mesh, the compost is usually held in place with sphagnum moss, but a network of more or less any fibrous material will do, as long as it will let water through and can be pulled aside so that plants can be inserted. Plastic netting is sometimes used, but this can look horrible, as can black polyetheline, which can be seen for weeks before the plants have grown enough to hide it. The moss need not be sphagnum. If you have a local source of wild moss, this will do just as well, but look for the stringy species rather than lumpy growths which could dry out and break up.

Compost is discussed at length on pages 122–123. Soilless compost is lighter and probably preferable for hanging baskets, but care must be taken to see that it *never* dries out.

PLANTING

The objective, although the container is hemispherical, is a perfect globe from which strands of dangling plants trail, giving the impression of a floral comet. The secret is to plant in layers.

ABOVE *Trailing forms of* Lobelia erinus, *available in a large number of different strains and shades of blue, mauve and white, are the most popular of all basket plants.*

RIGHT *The ultimate aim is for the hanging basket to grow to a generous globe shape. Here, a multicolored planting has produced exactly the right result without garishness.*

OPPOSITE *All ivy-leaf pelargoniums have the trailing habit so useful for hanging baskets. Floriferous varieties like red "Balcon Royale" are most effective on their own.*

Begin by lining the inside of the bottom of the basket with a little moss, then cover it with compost. Tease the roots of the lowest plants into the moss, and pull them gently through into the compost. Line a little more of the basket with moss, pour in more compost and plant another layer in the same way, repeating the process until you have reached the top. Put the final plants into the open top. Be sure to include some pendulous plants up there because you will want them to trail down and through the rest of the growth.

Do not worry if, when you have finished these maneuvers, the plants look a little dusty and bruised. Hang the basket on its hook, and water thoroughly. Then water again until the surplus flows through the bottom. Finally, using lukewarm water, syringe the foliage or sprinkle with a fine watering-can mist to wash off any compost. If you look after it, the basket should go on getting better and better for the next five months.

Winter or spring baskets Although hanging baskets are at their best in summer, it is possible, especially in milder areas, to prepare them in the fall for a spring display. The choice of plants hardy enough to come through a frosty winter is fairly limited, but, out of the wind and as long as the cold is not too extreme, wallflowers can make a handsome and fragrant display, particularly if blended with forget-me-nots.

Winter pansies, especially the Universal strain which has so many excellent pure colors, become pendulous with age and can be used to good effect, lasting on into summer if the blooms are removed and they are cut back from time to time and fed regularly. "Universal Apricot" and "Universal Blue" go particularly well together.

Do not feed in winter unless the weather is mild enough for growth to be sustained, but commence a weekly feed as soon as the weather warms up in spring and growth begins to accelerate.

As in all containers, ivy is a reliable standby which provides evergreen color, and can be backed up, in spring, with bulbs. Few work as well in hanging baskets as large Dutch crocuses, even though they are disappointingly short-lived. They must be planted with their noses pressed against the outside of the basket, so that the flowers break through the moss and bend upward as they bloom.

Summer baskets Many half-hardy container plants will grow in hanging baskets. Petunias thrive in them, and look well with *Helichrysum petiolare*. Ivy-leaved pelargoniums (geraniums) are natural for hanging baskets as are *Impatiens*, lobelia and the less rampant varieties of nasturtiums (*Tropaeolum majus*). These plants are often used in mixtures, the foliage making handsome backing for the flowers, but baskets can look every bit as sumptuous, and often more pleasing to the eye when planted with a single species.

Floriferous varieties of ivy-leaved pelargoniums, if fed and cared for, are smothered with bloom for months on end, and usually grow to form a perfect globe. Certain begonia species, such as the orange-flowered *Begonia sutherlandii*, can be used alone, and fuchsias, especially those with bicolored flowers, often look better on their own than "fussed up" with other plants.

Outlandish species deserve a trial too. Some of the ornamental oreganos, such as *Origanum rotundifolium* or *O.* "Barbara Tingey," have long-lasting, pendulous flower stems with subtle colorations. Grasses, especially those species with lank stems such as *Hakonechloa macra* "Albo-variegata" or the sedge *Carex flagellifera*, might be worth a try, and there is a pretty form of red clover with goldnetted leaves which would trail elegantly down the side of a basket. Indeed, any plant which has a pendulous habit, flowers for long periods and is happy to grow in relatively restricted soil is a potential basket case.

OPPOSITE *A wall furnished with wisteria may be dull after the spring blossom, but hanging baskets of summer flowers provide later color here with the climber as background.*

TROUGHS AND SINKS

ABOVE *Wild herb Robert,* Geranium robertianum, *has colonized this stone trough to excellent effect. Its leaves turn red when it meets with dry conditions, making a happy contrast with the bright emerald foliage of the wineberry,* Rubus phoenicolasius, *which is growing in the ground behind the trough. Herb Robert seeds freely.*

OPPOSITE *In this alpine garden set in a stone sink rocks are used to complement plants, which have been chosen to provide attractive colors and shapes all year. Note the dark sedum at the back, the silver artemisia at the far end, and the way plants have been encouraged to trail over the edges.*

Troughs and sinks are more frequently used for growing alpines than for anything else. In fact, they are just as good for any other kind of container gardening, but, because sinks provide such fine opportunities for growing a rock-plant collection, this seems as good a point as any to cover in detail what, after all, is an important aspect of container gardening.

The best-looking sinks are made of natural stone. Nowadays, old stone sinks are rare and expensive, but there are reasonably convincing fakes available, usually made of concrete which contains a high proportion of natural stone dust so that it adopts some of the natural color. When it has weathered and grown a little lichen, this material is almost indistinguishable from the real thing.

If you are not able to acquire a genuine stone sink, the next best material is porcelain. Old scullery sinks used to be beige or brown, with a rough glazing which looked reasonably mellow without further treatment, but the modern stark white is a little too unnatural unless coated with something to eliminate the dazzling quality of the ceramic surface. Alpine enthusiasts use "hyper tufa" for this: a sloshy mix of cement, peat and powdered tufa (page 49), which can be made to adhere to the sink surface by first molding wire mesh round the sides and then smearing the hyper tufa on top.

If tufa is unavailable, a mix of cement, brick dust and sand will do nearly as well, but will be darker in color. Another alternative is to make, or purchase ready made, "sinks" designed especially for housing alpines. Slate is a popular material, grooved and bolted together to the required dimensions, but there are other materials, mostly based on concrete.

Troughs are similar in use to sinks except that they are usually more capacious and therefore far heavier. A sink can, just, be moved about after planting; a trough has to stay put. As with sinks, stone is the most attractive material, but metal troughs can look perfectly acceptable, especially if they have become encrusted with limy deposits from the livestock's drinking water. Wooden troughs are also commonly used but never last as long.

Weathering is important, especially with new or recently installed troughs and sinks. Natural growths of moss, algae and lichen will arrive eventually, provided the surface is porous enough to support them, but their development can be hastened.

Yogurt is popular for this purpose; smear the stuff on the outer surface of the trough with a paintbrush. Smelly mixtures of manure and water are also recommended, but are extremely unpleasant to handle. A simple alternative is to apply liquid plantfood (page 128) with a watering-can. Whenever you feed other plants, remember to damp down the sides of the sink or trough with the same mixture.

One vital requirement for weathering, often overlooked by the experts, is the need for water. In high-rainfall areas, where the air is always charged with moisture, lichens multiply freely, and established walls or even tree trunks soon develop their own ecologies supporting not only moss but also ferns and epiphytic flowering plants. In drier climes, humidity can be pepped up with automatic watering systems, but a manual sprinkling, as often as you can remember, will help primitive life to gain a toehold on the stony surface.

Ivy, which clings to its climbing surfaces by producing a thick forest of adventitious roots, will attach itself more reliably if the stone is moist and if the moisture is enriched with plantfood from time to time.

When the trough or sink is in place, the next step, after insuring that drainage is adequate, is to fill it with the right compost. For alpines, drainage is crucial, but certain species will languish unless the soil is able to stay moist without waterlogging.

Loam, with its superior water-retentive properties (pages 122–123), is therefore an essential ingredient, and this needs to be combined with sharp grit or very coarse sand and also with peat. About a third by volume of each of these ingredients will provide a good general mix, but different species have their own preferences, so versatility and a willingness to compromise between different plant preferences are essential.

My own view is that rock plants look best set among rocks with the ground covered with a scree of grit or small gravel, imitating the type of stony debris found up a mountain. In a sink or trough, this is easy to do, providing you remember that space is limited. Too much enthusiasm for the miniature landscape may leave little room for the plants!

PLANTING

Two key factors must be considered as far as planting is concerned.

Scale Sinks and troughs planted with alpines are miniature gardens, so the plants need to be small. Introduction of anything out of scale will ruin the effect. Imagine a collection of miniature bulbs with a dozen huge hybrid tulips towering above them. By careful selection, it is possible to populate a trough with a collection of dwarf plants – even trees and shrubs – all in scale, without having to resort to bonsai.

Maintenance There are plenty of small plants which will survive for long periods without water. If the container is likely to be forgotten, or is in a part of the garden where watering is difficult, these are the plants to go for. The drawback is that most of them are not spectacular, particularly at times of year when

color is likely to run a little short. If you plan to water your trough regularly, be sure to go for one or two plants which will reward your pampering with a striking display. Incidentally, because they are usually smaller, sinks tend to dry out more quickly than troughs. Otherwise, the treatment can be much the same.

If planning a low-maintenance trough or sink, the all-season structure is particularly important. Dwarf conifers are useful here, but be sure the species you choose really are dwarf. *Juniperus communis* "Compressa," for example, is shaped like an exclamation point, and grows at the breathtaking rate of about $\frac{1}{2}$-inch a year, but there are other junipers which grow into big trees. The little holly *Ilex crenata* has several cultivars, stays small and can be clipped without losing its character, but, for evergreen foliage and deliciously aromatic spring flowers, *Daphne collina is* worthy of a place of honor in any trough, even though it dislikes extreme heat.

Deciduous dwarf shrubs include *Forsythia viridissima* "Bronxenses," whose spring twigs are smothered in yellow blooms but which never exceeds 2 feet. Some of the willows are surprisingly drought-resistant, and, even if they defoliate in a dry spell, will often revive after rain. *Salix* x *boydii* is especially pretty, and *Salix arbuscula* charming for growing over the sides of the trough.

As for the herbaceous plants, the most drought-tolerant are the sedums, sempervivums and jovibarbas. They all have fleshy leaves, but, unlike echeverias, are relatively frost-hardy and can be left out all year. Sedums are inclined to be invasive, but *Sedum kamtschaticum* "Variegatum" and S. *spathulifolium* are two with handsome flowers, foliage and excellent manners. There are hundreds of different rosette-forming sempervivums, all with interesting and variable leaf color ranging from maroon to emerald.

LEFT *Setting these sinks up on stones has brought the tiny plants closer to eye level.*

Underplanting these rugged little plants with bulbs will provide ephemeral flashes of beauty at certain times of the year. Several crocus species are especially happy in such harsh conditions. For spring or late winter color, for instance, *Crocus imperati is* gorgeous – its beige outer petals striped with chocolate and its flower center concealed until the sun opens the petals to reveal a violet interior with orange stigmata. The tiny *C. ancyrensis* throws up generous bunches of brilliant orange-yellow flowers at winter's end. In the fall, *C. speciosus* and even the fall-flowering snowdrop *Galanthus reginae-olgae* could be included to give the impression of a second spring.

If the trough is likely to get more attention, the range of colorful alpines which will thrive is almost endless. One of the advantages of troughs and sinks is that they can be elevated – on brick supports, for example – so that the little species can be enjoyed more easily. Close encounters with gentians or with alpine cranesbills reveal their exquisite forms.

Saxifrages, many of which are also drought-tolerant (as long as they do not get too hot), make perfect sink dwellers, the cushion types covered with jewel-like flowers in spring and the Aizöon group making neat, sometimes geometric rosettes, from which spring showy sprays of flowers, usually white. Finest of these is "Tumbling Waters" which, after taking several years to build up a big enough head of steam, explodes into a white cascade of bloom on a 24-inch spray.

As for bulbs, small narcissi look exquisite in troughs, but need a moisture-retaining soil and will tend to come blind after a few years unless conditions are kept damp enough. *Narcissus bulbocodium*, the "hoop petticoat" narcissus, is the easiest to grow, but there are a number of small hybrids which can be happy in a trough or sink. Anemones such as *Anemone blanda* make attractive companions for miniature narcissi. However, they tend to grow too large after flowering, so they would spoil the scale in a small sink.

All species of cyclamen, but not pot hy-

brids, are wonderful trough or sink plants. *Cyclamen persicum* is not hardy but is highly variable in color, ranging from pure white to deep pink, deliciously scented, and loves a summer bake. For cold areas C. *coum is* utterly hardy, and flowers with incredible valor during the coldest part of the year. All cyclamen have decorative foliage.

I have dealt almost exclusively with alpine gardening in this section on sinks and troughs, but do not forget that sinks and troughs make fine containers for other kinds of gardening, and are by no means the exclusive domain of the rock-garden enthusiast. The short section on tufa below is, however, strictly for alpinists.

TUFA

This soft stone is composed of porous lime-stone, and is formed when lime-laden water precipitates its calcium salts; stalagmites in caves are made of similar material. It is soft enough to be scraped or dug but hard enough to retain its shape. Being exceptionally porous, it absorbs water, and the way in which it is formed insures that it is richly decorated with galleries, holes and runs which are ideal for planting. A lump of tufa, the bigger the better, can make a fascinating feature if it is situated thoughtfully and well-planted.

Simply gouge a hole with a screwdriver to plant and cram the alpine in roots first, packing it with a little compost to get its roots started. European primulas, especially the tiny auricula types with leathery foliage, grow in tufa. Cushion and Aizöon saxifrages love it, and on the shady side, lime-loving ferns such as rustyback *(Asplenium ceterach* syn. *Ceterach officinarum)* or maidenhair spleenwort *(Asplenium trichomanes)* will grow happily.

OPPOSITE *A shallow sink, nicely lichened, blends comfortably into this rock garden.*

BELOW *The sink clad with hyper tufa makes a fine receptacle for* Diascia rigescens. *Its lax habit softens the hard upper edges.*

BALCONY BOXES

As the name suggests, balcony boxes belong exclusively on balconies. This is not as fatuous as it sounds: a balcony comes with its own special set of problems, making planning and skillful plant management essential.

Balconies are open on one side, often to the prevailing wind, and have solid structures at their backs. They may receive strong sunlight for part of the day but be in shadow for most of it; alternatively, they may face the sun all day without relief. And there may be privacy problems, with neighbors having too clear a line of vision for comfort.

When planning, remember the following key considerations.

Function Besides providing decoration, balcony boxes may be needed to provide shelter or shade. They must therefore be capacious enough to house the roots of tall plants or climbers, and also massive enough not to blow over in a storm.

Style If the balcony is the kind that Juliet leaned over to consort with Romeo, it will not look right with glossy fiberglass boxes, but it is difficult to create a mass of luxuriant foliage with nothing but a cluster of antique "terracottary." In addition, automatic watering systems are not always easy to link to old-fashioned containers. Thus, an old style may have to be imitated using modern materials. This is quite possible and will not detract from the effect any more than growing sixteenth-century style plants would spoil a modern balcony. In most cases there needs to be a compromise between functional requirements and aesthetically pleasing results. The health of the plants must come first, but, however fine the display, it would be ruined if the balcony-box designs were so obtrusive as to detract from the beauty of the plants.

PLANTING

Gardening a balcony may present practical difficulties. It may be laborious to water or service because, for example, sacks of compost have to be dragged up several flights of stairs. So the balcony box must earn its keep —

providing far more in the way of flowers and foliage than a counterpart playing a small role in a larger garden. In addition, color and interest must be maintained day after day. The quality of your planting design will be more severely tested here than in any other type of container gardening. There are two important principles to bear in mind now; see pages 62 and 64 for further advice on planting.

Levels It may seem obvious, but any successfully planted balcony will have different displays at different levels. Trees or climbers must be composed into groups at eye level and above; smaller shrubs or perennials should appear below them, while prostrate plants scramble between them and hang down the sides of the boxes. At each of those levels, a year-round range of colors, shapes, scents and textures must be considered but – and this is where it differs from gardening on a larger scale – there may only be room for a score or even fewer plants.

Off season Elsewhere, there may be room to carry plants purely for display at a particular time of year but, on a balcony, every plant must either look good for *most* of the time or must have several peaks. Small birch trees, for example, grown on Manhattan balconies have wonderful white trunks all the time, but their emerald-green spring foliage, emerging with such freshness, and their golden-yellow fall colors make them even more worthwhile. Pelargoniums (geraniums) are widely used because they flower all the time, and, in the tropics or sub-tropics, bougainvilleas flower almost perpetually.

Getting everything right the first time is seldom possible, even for a horticultural genius. But, because a balcony is so close to your living space and so compact, instead of taking 40 years, like Gertrude Jekyll adjusting her mixed borders, you can make effective changes from day to day. With careful handling, even mature plants can be transplanted and, since the total plant population is small,

ABOVE *This multicolored balcony proves that indiscriminate mixtures can be overpowering, though they brighten things up.*

OPPOSITE *Trailing silver helichrysum is used to enrich the foliage of a pink and white theme.*

you could probably purchase replacements for most of them without making too serious a dent in your finances.

Composing the planting of your balcony box or boxes should be a source of enjoyment. Bear all the preceding points in mind, but do not let any inhibitions prevent you from expressing your own tastes freely.

RAISED BEDS

A raised bed is about as large as a container gets. Balconies are seldom roomy enough to have them, but small town-gardens can be transformed by creating contained borders at different levels. Raised beds are especially useful in the following respects.

Light Increasing the height of the soil surface can enable plants to receive more daylight. This is helpful in gardens which are overshadowed by walls or neighboring buildings.

Maintenance Disabled people, especially if they are confined to a wheelchair, can often maintain raised beds, but would be unable to handle a garden at ground level. Special tools and aids are available these days to make wheelchair gardening easier. Raised beds are also far easier for able-bodied people to maintain because there is less bending to do.

Contouring A flat, boring site can be made more interesting by having raised beds at different levels.

Water features In tiny gardens, water features are often more effective if they are part of a system of raised beds. If a fountain or small brook can be made to run between two different levels, the feature is even more pleasing.

One problem with raised beds is that they often have ugly sides. To be strong enough to hold the soil in place, the walls must be constructed from heavy duty building materials. Whether these be manmade or of natural stone, they are, of necessity, so thick that it takes border plants longer to tumble and trail over their sides than it would in pots or boxes. Special attention must be paid, therefore, to the edges of raised beds, which should be planted so that as much of the sides as possible are concealed by growing material. Standing pots of plants in groups around the bases of the retaining walls can also help.

Raised beds can also present structural problems, especially if they have not been well-designed. The soil they contain is damp otherwise it would not support plant life – and when it freezes it expands. The stresses caused by the expansion of freezing soil can, at worst, cause cracking and eventual collapse in walls which are not damp-proofed, and at best whole sections of wall can shift or bulge, creating an unsightly outline. However, these disadvantages are so heavily outweighed by

OPPOSITE TOP *Raised beds in this white-theme garden enable trees to make a leafy tracery.*

OPPOSITE BOTTOM *In a raised bed large plants such as hollyhocks can grow to full size.*

BELOW *A dull corner is brought to life with boxes of foliage plants and a blue plumbago.*

the advantages of having raised beds that they should not discourage you. As far as the plants are concerned, a raised bed provides the best possible environment.

PLANTING

By their very nature, raised beds offer enormous scope for varied planting, and have a greater latitude for error. They hold a great deal of soil so the range of plants which will thrive in them is no more limited than in any conventional garden, and yet, because they are enclosed, it is possible to create a perfect micro-ecosystem.

For example, in an area where the soil is limy, a raised peat bed could make a home for camellias or azaleas, underplanted with gorgeous fall-flowering Asian gentians or with petiolarid primulas. Its fall foliage could be improved with the tiny *Sorbus reducta*, and the Chilean climber *Lapageria rosea* could be twined through the camellias, if the area is mild in winter, so that its red waxy flowers would contrast with their bottle-green foliage in late summer.

Raised beds offer better conditions for growing climbers than any other kind of container. This is because most climbers prefer a cool, moist rootrun. It is an advantage which should be exploited because vertical planting is important to any garden design.

Wherever there is an opportunity to plant a climber, consider growing two or three into one another. A climbing rose, for example, could carry one or two clematis so that the different flower shapes and colors contrast with each other. In partial shade, instead of selecting a single honeysuckle, think of putting in several: a *Lonicera periclymenum* "Belgica" plus "Serotina" for scent in spring and early summer, for example, intertwined with a *L.* x *brownii* for its late red color and a *L. japonica* "Halliana" to carry the exquisite perfume on into early winter. That way, there would be bloom, scent and greenery for almost ten months of the year. Climbers are covered in more detail on pages 78–81, 147–149.

OUTLANDISH CONTAINERS

Though some scoff at such whimsical notions, using peculiar receptacles for plants can be great fun. Wandering along the back streets of Oslo once, I discovered an ancient baby carriage, with fancy coachwork, wicker canopy and large, spoked wheels. But instead of housing a baby Norwegian, it contained pots of *Impatiens* and pelargoniums (geraniums). Elsewhere, in coastal resorts, I have seen a derelict open boat set up in the town center and planted with colorful half-hardy plants which cascaded over its sides. In rural towns and villages, an old farm cart is sometimes used for the same purpose.

Such plantings offer scope for humor, some of it unintentional, but there are also

ABOVE *The sempervivums seem to be thriving in these charming containers.*

opportunities for more serious artistic expression. The Norwegian carriage was delightful because the plants did not hide the attractive lines of the old vehicle, and I could enjoy the craftsmanship of a bygone age as well as reveling in the greenery. The flower-filled boats are in danger of becoming a cliché, but many vacationers, it seems, love them.

Chamber pots and antique bed-pans appeal to infantile senses of humor, but one sight that made me laugh out loud recently

was in a narrow alleyway in Lympstone, on Britain's Exe estuary. Outside the back door of a fisherman's cottage was a neat row of terracotta pots, all overflowing with lobelias and *Campanula isophylla*. Next to them, as if just vacated, was a pair of rubber boots, planted in the same way. "Everything round here gets planted," my companion explained. "He must have left his boots outside the door for more than five minutes!"

Whatever container you are considering using as a planter, there are three important points to bear in mind before you begin.

Aesthetics Rubber tires painted white or turned inside out, oil barrels, ammunition boxes and aluminum beer kegs are ugly. If they are used, be sure to hide them. A container should enhance the beauty of the plants it houses rather than distract the eye.

Suitability If the container looks too out of place in your garden or on your balcony, abandon it. A genuine, time-expired wheelbarrow planted up with begonias might look acceptable in a country garden, but a fake, wrought-iron affair would be far too cute. In a stylish town plot the reverse might be true — it depends on your point of view!

Practicality However outlandish, a container must contain enough compost to support growing plants, must drain freely and must be stable enough not to collapse or blow over in a gale. If there is only room for very little compost, plant with rock dwellers which will enjoy such an austere habitat.

One of the most common concepts in garden design is that of Nature juxtaposed with Art. High-flown, you might think, but to me it simply means that fancy structures are prettier when intertwined with growing plants: the romantic ruin bedecked with fragrant old rambling roses or covered in ivy is always popular. So, fine though the handiwork may be, I believe that any container is all the better for a mix with Mother Nature.

ABOVE *Container or statue? The main attraction is in the stonework here, so planting needs to be minimal. The sedum planted in the cornucopia is exactly right.*

ABOVE RIGHT *A retired boat makes a jolly home for hyacinths. After spring, summer annuals could take their place, provided the container drains adequately.*

RIGHT *A delightful group of sempervivums grows in an old upturned roofing tile in little more than a spoonful of soil. In such harsh conditions the plants develop their colors and textures to perfection.*

THE
CONTAINED
GARDEN

Sometimes from choice, but more often from necessity, an entire garden or outdoor growing area is containerized, and nothing grows directly in the ground.

There are several reasons for growing everything in containers, the most common being that gardening any other way would be impossible. If the garden is on a roof or balcony, for example, there will be no natural ground. Elsewhere, the earth may be too stony, chalky or barren for growing plants. Or there may be too little space for any but the most economical planting.

Besides the physical limitations, there are often environmental problems which make growing difficult unless containers are used. Neighboring high buildings, for example, may create deep shade, restricting the choice of plants, and can even cause wind effects which may be too severe for conventional garden planting.

In this chapter, I look at the various possibilities open to contained gardeners, including gardening vertically and growing fruit and vegetables, and examine several different kinds of settings in detail.

LEFT *These grouped containers placed against a background of luxuriant climbers are planted with sedum, zonal and trailing pelargoniums, a tall agapanthus and dotted with French marigolds to provide color throughout summer and fall.*

USING CONTAINERS

There is no need to see contained gardens as a poor second choice to conventional growing. They offer as much scope for excellence as any other gardening activity. After all, if the Dutch barge owners can make their boats so attractive, not just with bright paintwork but with tubs and boxes full of thriving plants, we should be able to do something with even the tiniest space.

The potential of even the smallest, dingiest outdoor area will surprise you. Flowers, if the right varieties are selected, can be induced to perform in dense shade or in a bleak corner; surprisingly large trees can be grown for decades in containers without coming to any harm and without becoming nuisances. Food – not just a few pot herbs but fruit and vegetables – can be raised in tubs and pots; indeed for some crops, such as early strawberries, pot culture is a positive advantage.

Whether conventional or containerized, successful garden design depends on the same basic principles. These were covered in some detail on pages 10–15, but it is worth emphasizing that to achieve a skeleton or framework of plants which maintains interest all year takes even more careful planning than in conventional gardens.

The big advantage of the contained garden is that you have more versatility because containers can be moved about or replaced from time to time during the year. Perhaps their biggest single disadvantage is that the ultimate size of the largest plants – trees and shrubs especially – will almost certainly have to be restricted, either because no container will be large enough to accommodate their root systems without cramping, or because they would otherwise become too big for their chosen site.

ABOVE *On some sites – such as this Dutch barge – gardening would be completely impossible without containers.*

LEFT *Harsh lines in this roof garden have been softened by planting trailing roses and siting a hosta for lush foliage.*

OPPOSITE *Even in roof gardens, a luxuriant effect can be created by massing containers and planting them with vigorous growers.*

In small gardens this is unlikely to pose a problem because you probably will not want big trees, but in larger sites it is frustrating to discover that trees cannot achieve their optimum natural size because of the restriction of their root systems. There are various ways in which the health and size of the trees in a contained garden can be maintained at optimum levels, and these are covered in the section on roof gardens (pages 64–73).

In a conventional garden, if you want to make changes, you must dig plants up and even make new beds, whereas in the contained garden, ringing the changes could mean no more than shuffling a few pots around. Whether or not you are the restless type who likes to keep shifting things, a major part of the job of running a contained garden is the acquiring of containers.

The permanent kind are usually once-only purchases, and may even be built in. Whether they consist of raised beds, large boxes or troughs, they will probably make up the basis of the skeleton planting. Trees in large tubs and hedges, or bushes in raised beds or boxes, are too cumbersome or heavy to move more than once in a while, but as far as the temporary planting is concerned, variety can be effected by a steady stream of additions, subtractions or relocations.

It is especially important, therefore, to have a supply of small pots and urns to furnish the lower edges of large containers and to soften the outlines. Boxes which hold trees can be underplanted, or covers can be fitted so that these can carry plants needing different soil conditions, or simply to use as work surfaces; such covers must either be permeable to water or detachable to facilitate watering. Tiny containers, the type which would hold houseplants indoors, can also be incorporated into the contained garden, as tabletop ornaments or to fill gaps.

Since most of these containers will be placed in prominent positions, it is worth looking out for something special. If you see one you like, grab it, even if it threatens to cost an arm and a leg. You will not regret it.

Alas, antique examples are rare and expensive these days, and modern terracotta seems not to have the lasting properties of the old material. However, imitations and more durable materials mellow eventually (pages 33, 44,

45). Metal pans, wooden boxes, blackened earthenware or half-glazed pots are all examples of desirable planters which can be made to look delightful.

Because most contained gardens are small and nearly always close to or adjoining the main reception rooms of the house or apartment, it is essential that functional and aesthetic factors are not allowed to cancel each other out. Vegetable crops must look pretty as well as be productive; a screen which keeps the wind off or turns prying eyes away must also be beautiful; trees positioned to provide shade and coolness in the garden must have outlines which look beautiful from inside the building, and so on.

Bearing these general points in mind, I will now look at some typical sites ripe for the development of a contained garden.

ABOVE *It may not be possible to grow much in the ground in this gravelly yard, but the space has been enlivened with half-tubs of clipped evergreens in a formal arrangement. Their position can be changed at any time.*

ABOVE *This roof garden is furnished with inexpensive containers – half oil-drums – planted for exuberant growth and high color. Roses need feeding throughout the growing season to grow so large.*

BALCONY GARDENS

Balcony boxes and their planting are covered on pages 50–51, but where there is a room, a balcony can become almost a garden.

A surprisingly luxuriant effect can be achieved if the containers are well-placed and judiciously planted. Freestanding trees or bushes in tubs or pots will add to the general mass of greenery, and these can be under-planted by placing small pots at their feet or by growing low and trailing plants in the tubs.

Walls at the backs of balconies are often neglected, but wall-mounted brackets to carry semicircular planters or halfbaskets can transform otherwise dull expanses of wall. If the site is too shady for most flowering plants, it may still be suitable for ferns or even for epiphytic orchids.

Many of the suggestions covered in the next section, on roof gardens, also relate to balconies, but, unlike some roof gardens, most balconies are narrow and one-sided, which restricts the use of large trees and makes it difficult to create shade except by using climbers on narrow screens. If one of the strong points of the balcony is its view – out over the ocean, say, or across a city landscape – care must be taken to avoid obstructing it with too much greenery. Partial screening can help: erect a trellis for climbers only at the wind-ward end of the balcony, or over a small part of it. A narrow screen or strategically planted evergreen can be surprisingly effective.

In such a small space, the furniture is a crucial part of the design and planting must be subordinate to it. Positioning fragrant plants near the heads of sitters will make the experience of being on the balcony pleasurable, but if your visitor pokes her eye on a badly placed *Cordyline australis* when she leans forward to take a pretzel, you will be sorry, especially when you hear from her lawyer.

ABOVE *Containers on even the tiniest balcony bring nature into the heart of the city.*

OPPOSITE *A balcony garden corner is made discreet by standing pots on the parapet.*

ROOF GARDENS

It seems pretty obvious that a roof garden is bound to be a contained garden. Since there will be no soil on the roof, unless the house happens to be an underground bunker, whatever the plants grow in must have been put there. But in spite of this highly artificial situation, roof gardens can look amazingly natural – even jungle-like – if they are well designed and properly planted.

There are several practical problems to consider as you plan your design.

Weight Gardens can be heavy, especially if the plants are growing in mineral soil in large stone or concrete containers. If surplus weight is likely to damage the roof or jeopardize safety, perhaps a roof garden is not such a good idea. But even if the roof is load-bearing, it is sensible to reduce the weight. One way is to use soilless compost. Peat is light and bulky, but increases its weight enormously when saturated with water.

Damp It is essential to insure that the building is suitable for a roof garden. Plants must be in containers which drain freely. If the design of the roof is unsuitable, this could lead to serious problems. Whereas rainwater runs harmlessly off an empty roof, the presence of planters could hold water back during storms or help to cause snow-drifts which might result in seepage. In addition, using an automatic watering system on a leaky roof is bound to cause damage to the apartment beneath.

ABOVE RIGHT *Few roof gardens can boast a Manhattan skyline, but a patch of greenery in any city is sure to be life-enhancing.*

RIGHT *Bright, formal pelargoniums will maintain summer color, but for structure the tree in the background has been pruned to a shape which will look good all year.*

OPPOSITE *Plenty of variety gives a city roof garden a lush effect. There is even a fruiting cherry tree!*

Light Contrary to what you might think, many roof gardens are as overshadowed as ground-level urban gardens and, if there is excessive shading, the choice of plants will be restricted accordingly. This is not a damaging limitation, but it does call for more careful selection when devising the planting scheme.

Wind Roof gardens are often windy, so much of the planting will need to be wind-resistant. Barriers which minimize the effect of the wind may be necessary.

HOUSING LARGE PLANTS

Unlike balconies or small terraces, some roof gardens are roomy enough to accommodate quite large trees. The principles of cultivation apply as much here as to a 5-inch pot, except that the tree is unlikely to grow to its full potential size, even though there may be plenty of room for it in the roof garden. To minimize the risk of growing trees which fail to reach a desirable size, and to insure that they stay as healthy as possible and retain their attractive shapes, the following rules are worth observing.

Container size Use as large a container as is practicable. Various physical constraints will limit the size you select, but it is important to give the roots as long a run as is possible.

Stability Make sure the container is stable. Wind leverage on the top of the tree could blow the container over.

Feeding Feed regularly but do not overfeed. (See pages 128–129 for recommendations.) With mature trees, an annual feed treatment will suffice, but if the tree shows signs of starvation, with yellowing and undersized foliage, give a foliar feed or an extra liquid feed directly into the container.

Watering Water copiously. As the tree develops, the container will become rootbound, and will dry out astonishingly quickly. Be especially vigilant during hot weather when the tree will be emitting moisture at a rapid rate, using a lot of water in a short time.

Pruning Prune if you can do so without ruining the shape of the tree. Tips on pruning are given on page 130.

DESIGN

Roof gardens can be put to a variety of uses, and the design style you choose will be determined very largely by how you decide to use the space. As a place in which to relax, a garden on the roof can be as good as any other garden. For plant collectors who delight in building up their stocks of special rarities, there are some limitations because not everything lends itself to container culture, but there still remain thousands of species which are as much at home in rooftop containers as in their native mountains, forests or meadows. Alpines, for example, can be grown to a decent size and featured in their own freestanding pots, and the lovely Japanese maple *Acer palmatum* "Atropurpureum" – a highly collectible variety – makes a wonderful shape, and has lovely deep purple foliage.

For low-maintenance gardens, where automatic watering is unavailable, collections of plants which enjoy arid conditions can be amassed. Pans or pots containing sempervivums, echeverias, sedums or cacti will all survive for ages without much attention, and many produce attractive flowers. In hot climates, bougainvilleas will flower with next to no water.

A roof garden can also be used to grow food crops, but this subject will be covered at some length on pages 82–84.

Supposing that you want a garden to relax in, and remembering the advice given on pages 10–11 about knowing your style, just how do you effect a passable imitation of, say, a glade or a formal eighteenth-century ornamental garden on top of a tower block?

For a formal style, boxes and tubs can be lined up and planted to replicate a variety of patterns very successfully. As long as the plants all grow and flower at roughly the same size and rate, the symmetry of the arrangement will be maintained. Even flat surfaces which are not especially pretty can be enhanced by standing pots, or even flat pans, planted very simply at regular intervals. Outdoor furniture fits into such landscaping with considerable ease because formal garden design has so much in common with interior design. Sometimes a large plant can become almost part of the furniture. For example, a clipped tree could have a circular table constructed around it so that it acts as a table decoration at the same time as providing natural, dappled sunshade for sitting in.

ABOVE *Containerized trees in roof gardens can grow surprisingly large. In such a situation a raised bed offers the best possible rootrun. The other requirements for a healthy, happy tree are regular feeds, generous watering and sensitive pruning.*

ABOVE *Bush and climbing roses have been planted in this roof garden to grow up and conceal part of the brickwork. The container holding the pink rose is partially hidden by a strategically placed variegated hosta, making a lovely plant association.*

For a natural landscape style, the task is to build up the plant collection until there is such an abundance of greenery that hard edges have all but disappeared. Every angle, wall, and even the edges of the containers themselves must be furnished with living material. Using such large and unruly plants as *Onopordon acanthium*, the cotton-thistle, or free-seeding opium poppies will help to enhance the "wild" and "woolly" effect reminiscent of an open tract of land.

The advantage of creating an informal garden is that, although a sound plan is nonetheless essential for year-round interest as well as spring and summer climaxes, it is possible to make small changes here and there adding plants or taking them away – at any time of year without spoiling the overall effect in any way. Creepers can be encouraged to grow into and intertwine with standing bushes or trees, and bowls or pots of interesting specimen plants can be brought into the garden both with no fear whatsoever of upsetting the symmetry of the display.

On the other hand, it may not always be easy to keep an informal planting under control. What appears as a delightful exuberance of growth one day, can go out of control and become a mess the next. While the formal gardener is lifting spring forget-me-nots out of well-ordered boxes to replace them with petunias – all done in a morning – the informal gardener has to decide whether to leave them to go to seed or pull them up, spoiling perhaps a delightful grouping of white variegated honesty and the young blue-gray foliage of the opium poppy, both of which were allowed to seed themselves along the tops of the boxes the previous year.

Whether the style is formal or informal, close attention needs to be paid to color. Because roof gardens, like most other contained gardens, are usually small and intimate, any mistake is all the more apparent. Remember, for example, that informal gardens offer scope for a wide color range, but too many different hues in a small area inevitably will result in a restless effect.

TOP *Trailing plants, lilies and marigolds make this half tub a good focal point.*

ABOVE *Varnished wood containers, planted with pinks and reds, warm a gray parapet.*

LEFT *Different levels, dense planting and a water feature transform this roof space.*

ABOVE *This informal assortment of containers is surprisingly effective. The plants, which include rockroses, lilies, roses and even rapid annuals like opium poppies, will provide a succession of color for several months. However, some of the colors are rather startling and might clash.*

RIGHT *Boisterous plants with harmonious color characterize this splendid roof garden. There is plenty to come – hydrangeas and Shasta daisies, for example – and the structural planting, using shrubs, has been masterly and will maintain winter interest.*

Roof gardens vary enormously in proportion, but, because they are often an afterthought rather than an integral part of the building design, their shape and aspect are seldom ideal. With careful planning, however, small, irregular spaces can be a positive advantage because they present opportunities to increase the "mystery value" of the garden. Exciting design is often the result of having to confront and overcome a particular awkwardness about a site.

Imagine, for example, an L-shaped site with a small, narrow passage forming the lesser part. By planting screens of fragrant climbers on either side of the narrow part and placing a seat at its center, a cramped, dismal space can be turned into a secluded scented bower. If there is room, a quartet of well-placed urns or perhaps a statue could even create a little vista (pages 91–95).

Dividing an area with screens of living or manufactured material and leading paths around them can give an impression of size; so can paths winding around large objects such as trees or groups of shrubs. Mirrors have also been used to good effect – to double the width or length of whatever is in their view – but they tend to go shabby outdoors after a while and lose their reflective quality.

Creating a *trompe l'œil* with trelliswork can make a flat screen look as though it has porticoes and arches. It is just a question of angling the slats on the trellis in such a way that the perspective suggests three dimensions when there are, in fact, only two. Growing climbing roses on the trelliswork is a decorative way of maintaining the illusion.

Often, there are ugly features which need hiding, such as an air vent, a chimney stack or the coping of a wall. Do not automatically go for the obvious solutions of growing creepers over them or placing groups of shrubs around them. Is the object itself less ugly than the bunching of plants which would hide it? It may be more effective to lay out the roof garden ignoring the ugly feature, but making sure that wherever possible the eye is distracted by some more pleasing focal point.

Strategic positioning of a statue, a seat, an especially striking specimen plant or a water feature can help here, making a centerpiece at the end of a vista or with other plants arranged to lead the eye to it. Even very shallow, still water in a raised pond will reflect its surroundings and give a feeling of depth. Moving water, such as fountains or streams, needs a little more depth and, on a small scale, is in danger of looking "fussy," but it can be used to excellent effect.

At night, a roof garden is usually small enough to light completely. Low-level lighting creates wonderful shadows and shapes not seen during the day when the light is supplied by the gentleman upstairs. There are those who delight in the use of colored illuminations, but artificial colors drain plant material of its natural shades and something important is therefore lost.

Although some roof gardens do boast lawns, the notion of a lawn mower going up and down once a week, on top of a city tower block, is very bizarre. Flooring is more usual, and is generally constructed of wooden decking, through which water can pass freely and find its way to the building's drainage system, or of tiles or slates.

The *illusion* of a lawn would not be difficult to create, however, using prostrate plants such as wild thyme, *Thymus serpyllum*, or, in frost-free climates, the dangerously invasive *Soleirolia soleirolii* (syn. *Helxine soleirolii)* or even chamomile, though the latter has to be trimmed from time to time. Thyme needs next to no soil, and can be grown in shallow trays which soon knit together. Although such a construction is not suitable to walk on, it can create a softening feature which, in summer, changes from green to purple or bright pink or white, or a mixture of these colors as the plants come into flower.

A lovely Victorian alternative to this idea is carpet bedding. Frowned on by the plantsmen, because it causes the plants to lose their individuality, and falling out of favor in parks and gardens because of the high labor input, this technique consists of planting dense masses of slow-growing, low material in a specific pattern – creating, in other words, a tapestry picture out of living plants. Echeverias, sempervivums, gold-leaved feverfew and *Anthemis cretica* subsp. *cupaniana* are only a few of the plants used for carpet bedding. Some have to be clipped from time to time, to maintain "picture definition," and a single weed would be anathema.

ABOVE *Climbing plants like this* Parthenocissus *make attractive screens, but need a cool rootrun and must be fastened securely, especially in exposed sites.*

OPPOSITE *A mirror has been used here to create a* trompe l'œil, *giving the impression of a long vista. Note how the brightly colored* Impatiens *highlights the shaded area.*

TERRACES AND FRONT GARDENS

ABOVE *Even a front door which opens onto the street has room for plants in containers, as this exuberant garden amply demonstrates.*

ABOVE *Formal pots containing clipped evergreens, flanked here by rhododendrons, create a dignified entrance.*

Frequently, house frontages have only a small terrace or paved area separating them from the street. It is nearly always possible to create a minute garden in this restricted area, but working at ground level may not be the most effective approach. If containers are used, they can add to the height by bringing up the level of the soil, and so increase the range of plants which can be grown.

If a formal theme is in order, stylish urns and planters can be placed to provide elegant decorations which enhance the house. Iron palings, balustrading or low fencing are sometimes used, but can look too forbidding unless they are decorated with living material.

However formal the design is, permanent plantings of "trailers" such as ivy or *Parthenocissus* will help to soften some of the lines. Subsequent additions depend very much on personal taste. English gardeners tend to go for a mix of colors which is not always restful. Discerning American gardeners are far more strict about their color choice, and will devise a scheme which has more in common with an interior decor – pure white azaleas, perhaps, with nothing more than marbled ivy to back them up.

Few front gardens provide perfect conditions, but some present almost too much of a challenge. Specific problems obviously

ABOVE *At this front door, the severity of the clipped evergreens has been softened with summer flowers, including nasturtiums.*

ABOVE *The harsh lines of a tiny area have been transformed with a riot of pansies, petunias, pelargoniums,* Impatiens *and fuchsias.*

require specific recommendations, but in general terms the way to cope is first to identify the problems, and then to select the right plants to minimize the undesirable effects. A roadside sidewalk which is splashed with salty slush in winter and covered with dust in summer may seem a hopeless case, but there are plants which will tolerate salt spray. Shrubs such as *Fuchsia magellanica,* tamarisk, cordyline and *Cytisus,* for example, enjoy salty air.

Whatever the scheme chosen, it is worth remembering that a front terrace in a street is part of the public domain, and tells outsiders more about you and your tastes than they could possibly learn from your drapes or the state of your paintwork. However, a front terrace is also seldom a place for lingering, so the artistic objective must be to create a swift impact rather than waste time on subtleties which nobody will have time to notice.

On a private back terrace, your approach can be more relaxed. Sitting over a drink or a barbecue, there will be time to enjoy carefully chosen color contrasts, different textures of leaf or a comprehensive collection of Aizöon saxifrage species – or all three. In short, then, your garden must be designed according to *your* needs, but, however private the rear may be, bear in mind that front gardens are usually under public scrutiny.

STEPS

The chances are that there is at least one change of level in your garden and therefore that you have steps. How well-designed are they and, more to the point, how well-furnished? Any stairway, from antique hand-carved limestone to a disused metal fire escape, can be improved by strategic positioning of plants in containers.

Imagine an external stairway with pots of orchids arranged in cascades down either side, or a metal balcony and stairs festooned with colorful climbers and trailers. The different levels make for a fine display, especially if plants are carefully selected so that some tumble down, others rear up and the two kinds intermingle.

Remember, however, that unobstructed, free passage is essential. At no time should you compromise safety with Art! Fire escapes must not be obstructed, and flights of steps must, at all times, be passable with ease. Observing such rules is merely common sense, but a large area of most stairways, unless they are exceptionally narrow or winding, is never used and affords space enough for plants.

For some, steps down to a basement apartment may be all the garden they have, in which case it is essential to maximize its potential. But steps down to any restricted area can be made beautiful with plants in containers. Climbing plants will enjoy growing in the cool in pots below street level, especially if they can reach for the sun up stairway banisters. *Impatiens* can be relied on to flower in the gloom below and, if boxes or planters are fixed to the banister rails, the whole area can erupt into masses of brilliant color or a torrent of soft greenery, depending on your taste.

ABOVE *Flowers are not always necessary. There is a huge choice of foliage plants offering subtle variations of hue and form. Many tolerate deep shade and are evergreen.*

RIGHT *Mixing flower colors needs care. Soft tones can almost disappear in the face of the bolder reds and yellows.*

OPPOSITE *An imposing entrance is here decorated with color and formal shapes. The topiary could be moved elsewhere in summer when the other plants are most colorful.*

VERTICAL GARDENING

The importance of vertical gardening, especially in a contained garden, cannot be overstressed. Imagine a small urban garden with room perhaps for a little table, some chairs, a tiny raised bed and some pretty groups of containers. Now surround that space with a wall on all sides. It does not take a mathematical genius to work out that those vertical surfaces represent a considerable additional area. Without good wall cover, the garden's potential has not been thoroughly exploited.

PLANTING

A well-furnished wall is one which is completely covered by an exciting range of plants chosen to offer some flower or leaf interest through every month of the year. In conventional gardens, where soil is deep, growing climbers and wall plants pose no problems at all. For containers, however, the choice will need a little more thought. Most plants will be happy, especially if they receive extra feed and water – advice on caring for climbers is given on page 130 – but a few are unlikely to perform as well as they would in the ground.

The most vigorous rambling roses, for example, usually fail to reach their full potential, and will tend to look half-starved, and make other plants with which they share a container look half-starved too. Since they frequently have the added disadvantage of flowering only once a year, they are not the ideal candidate for this type of planting. The slower climbing roses, on the other hand, are excellent in containers, and flower all the better for a little root discipline. In warm areas, the delectable Victorian and Edwardian Tea roses – varieties like the apricot "Lady Hillingdon" or the creamy "Sombreuil" – enjoy container life, as does the blood-red, headily fragrant "Guinée." Hundreds of modern climbing roses are equally suitable, and provide a full color range to choose from.

Of clematis, the montana kind is difficult to discipline, and may overwhelm your planting design but, if fast-growing, dense cover is needed, it may be worthwhile. The finest white cultivar is *Clematis chrysocoma* var. *sericea* and, if you can find the true species, *C. chrysocoma* is the softest shell pink. Both plants have well-shaped flowers, and last for several weeks. Some large-flowered clematis take exception to being container-grown, especially when their roots are not kept cool, but they are in the minority, leaving about two hundred good-natured varieties from which to select.

My special favorites are the late flowering *Clematis viticella* cultivars. They have smaller flowers than the large hybrids, but are smothered with color from midsummer to late fall, and you can cut them back to ground level in late winter, getting rid of all those hideous naked stems. The wild species with its small, dark-blue flowers is a bit low-key, but the cultivar "Alba Luxurians" has dazzling white flowers with a hint of blue, and each sepal is edged with green foliage frills. "Minuet" is a wonderful purple with a white center, and "Rubra" a gorgeous port-wine red, which contrasts rather sumptuously with yellow or lemon roses.

Besides roses, clematis and honeysuckle (pages 147–149), there are hundreds of other climbers which make rapid growth and provide fast cover or shade. Bougainvilleas, jasmines, *Allamanda*, *Lapageria* and *Ipomoea* are all examples for warm countries. In frosty areas we can select such lovely genera as *Akebia*, *Wisteria*, *Ampelopsis*, *Humulus* (hops), *Hydrangea*, *Vitis* (grapevines) and, if we are foolhardy or desperate, the dreaded Russian bindweed, *Polygonum baldschuanicum*.

OPPOSITE *Vertical surfaces often make up a significant portion of the "gardenable" area. Here, almost every square inch has been put to good use. On the ground, containers, planted with dahlias and other herbaceous plants, jostle for space. Behind them fuchsias and climbers have been encouraged to cover the wall, which is not only furnished with a wooden trellis but also carries a number of well-filled planters.*

ABOVE *A line of containers planted with the normally climbing* Schizophraga *has been set out to create a thick, leafy screen which, as well as looking attractive, deadens sound and improves privacy. Most wall shrubs and even ivy can be grown this way, but it requires patience and skillful training.*

OPPOSITE *An arbor, with bars supported by brick columns, has been planted with vines which will soon scramble over the top, creating shade. The standard daisy bush helps to bridge the gap between the low containerized plants and the climbers.*

Climbers vary in their vigor, so it is important to plant the right ones together, not only to insure a pleasing color and texture grouping but also to prevent one species from swamping the rest. Where climbers are grown into shrubs, it is often prudent to select plants which can be cut hard back – *Clematis viticella*, for example, or herbaceous climbers such as *Asarina erubescens* (syn. *Maurandya erubescens*), *Eccremocarpus scaber*, or the enchanting climbing monkshood, *Aconitum volubile* – so that the outline of the host shrub is rescued each season before it is engulfed.

Wall cover is not the only form of vertical gardening for the contained garden. Plant screens can play an invaluable part in providing decorative shelter or some of the "soft-landscape" structures used in garden design. Substantial plants are required, or a sturdy trellis or frame which is strong enough to support a fully grown climber in rain or wind. The same principles apply to planting screens as to planting for wall cover except that screens lack the shelter often provided by a wall, and this may limit the choice of plants.

The alternative to a trellis is a hedge. In the contained garden, a perfectly good hedge can be grown in a raised bed or box, or even in a row of large pots. Most kinds of hedge plant can be grown in containers, and have the added advantage of being movable. For a formal effect, there are hundreds of species which are happy to be clipped, but of these the traditional yew, holly, box and cypress are among the best. Clipping is usually an annual event, but the fineness of the clip and level of formality depend on personal preference. Topiary has a large number of uses in formal gardening, and is discussed on pages 132–133.

Informal hedging screens are just as easy to contrive, but it should be remembered that an unpruned shrub will be more open in habit, and therefore make a less effective screen than will a close-clipped hedge. Informal plantings of mixed shrubs allow for a greater range of color and texture, however, and can be underplanted with cottage-style herbaceous subjects to create a "wild" look.

CONTAINER CROPS

Growing your own food is fun. Some people love the primeval feel of being able, at least in part, to feed themselves from their own resources. The fact that the salad or beans came from your own patch means that, even if you have not grown them organically, at least you know exactly which chemicals you have used.

In the contained garden, growing food is not only perfectly possible, but is widely practiced. However, you must remember that, compared with a complete kitchen garden, growing fruit and vegetables in pots or tubs has its limitations, and with cropping, as an alternative to ornamental gardening, there are several important considerations.

Yield For maximum yield, most vegetables and fruits need full light. Therefore, in a well-planned, attractive garden where some shade is essential, optimum yields are unlikely.

Aesthetics Vegetable crops, even in the most artistically planned French potager, often fall short of the beautiful. Brussels sprouts, for example, look gaunt and forlorn, especially at mid-harvest, and dying squash plants have less appeal than discarded newspapers.

Space Two problems here. First, vegetable crops tend to hog a lot of ground. A single cabbage, at maturity, can cover an area of 1 square yard. Second, when the crop is harvested, it leaves an ugly gap which, in a kitchen garden, poses no problems, but in a small contained garden can ruin the effect.

These factors have been presented as disadvantages, but they are not insurmountable and indeed, with care and skill, can be turned into advantages.

The simplest way to maximize yield is to abandon the flowers, and concentrate exclusively on the crops, using fertilizers and pesticides and keeping the whole garden scrupulously weed-free. That way, the vegetable output will be huge, but, unless you are a frustrated arable farmer, you will be dissatisfied with the way your garden looks. To obtain a reasonable yield but still have a pretty garden, you must compromise.

Feed the vegetables as much as you can without making the flowers grow rank and coarse. Select varieties for their looks as well as their productivity, and, above all, site plants sympathetically. When vegetable crops are lifted and leave gaps, these must be planted up as soon as possible either with other vegetables or with fast-growing flowers – hardy annuals, perhaps, or pot-grown plants already in flower.

As far as aesthetics are concerned, there may not be much you can do about the looks of an exhausted calabrese plant other than to pull it up, but healthy vegetables do have a beauty all their own. The fresh, ferny effect of young carrot leaves, the glowing red of tomatoes, the funereal purple-black of eggplants and the cool blue-green of brassica and leek foliage are all features which would grace any garden, however sensitively planted. A friend of mine grows broccoli, and allows it to flower because he says he loves the lemon yellow of the blooms! So, selecting vegetable species with visual appeal is a good first step toward overcoming any artistic shortcomings.

Association will do the rest. Growing ornamental plants alongside the crops will help to compose a pleasing picture. Among your collection of climbers, for example, scarlet runner beans make a charming contribution with their emerald foliage and bright red flowers. While you are about it, why not include a cucumber or two, some gourds and a melon? Even large squashes can be trained to run up screens and blend in with other climbers, although their heavy fruits may need extra support to prevent them from dragging the vines down with their weight.

At ground level, dwarf tomatoes among the summer bedding will provide color when in fruit, and, if there is room, globe artichokes are worthy of a place of honor anywhere, especially varieties with silvery foliage. Leave a bloom or two to develop because when the scaly part opens, the flower is bright blue.

There have always been oddly colored varieties of commonplace vegetables in the seed catalogs, but in recent years, with revived interest in kitchen gardens, the number of vegetables which are grown as much for their beauty as for their taste has increased enormously.

ABOVE *A fine crop of containerized scarlet runners, establishing an excellent temporary screen against a wall in a rather bleak site. The dahlias, pelargoniums and lobelia planted among them add extra and contrasting color, resulting in a happy blend of beauty and utility.*

RIGHT *Vegetables will thrive in containers, provided growing conditions are ideal. They take up a lot of room, but a well-ordered kitchen garden, even in a limited space, can be surprisingly productive. Pansies and cabbages make an odd match!*

Ornamental cabbages and kales are highly colorful, and can be left to go to seed or harvested for the pot. Some of their colors are a bit loud, especially the lurid pink variety, but they have often been used to create startling bedding schemes. Other fancy members of the cabbage family include purple cauliflowers such as "Winter Cape," red Brussels sprouts ("Rubine") and various unusual calabrese, such as "Rosalind" (red) and "Romanesco" (yellow).

Beans and peas come in several colors. Pea flowers are pretty enough in the conventional white form, but there are peas with purple flowers and purple pods. Runner bean flowers are white, scarlet or shades in between the two.

One leafy vegetable of great beauty is rhubarb chard, which has dark purple leaves and scarlet stems, but the common chard, with its huge, crinkled leaves held erect and snow-

ABOVE *The strawberry's handsome foliage looks beautiful most of the year.*

OPPOSITE *All citrus species boast evergreen foliage, rich scent and colorful fruits.*

white stems, is almost as decorative. Lettuce and chicory come in all shades, shapes and sizes from deep green through rusty bronze to red, and other salad greens, especially corn salad, Florence fennel and colored celery, are all decorative and useful plants.

FANCY FRUIT

Most fruit trees are so attractive that they seldom pose artistic problems, even in a contained garden. Top fruit — fruit from trees — can be grown successfully in containers. Indeed, the traditional nineteenth-century orchard house was designed to house fruit trees in tubs that stood outdoors in summer, but were brought in under glass to force in winter, so that, with heat and constant care, fresh apples or pears could be ready by late spring. Cherries, pears and apples all make pretty container trees with lovely spring blossom. Pruning may have to be adapted slightly to keep the trees small and the shape attractive, but they will still bear fruit.

Peaches, apricots, plums and nectarines make beautiful wall plants which, fan-trained, will yield plenty of fruit, as well as having ornamental blossom and lovely foliage. Figs also thrive on a warm wall, producing large, high-value fruits. In warm climates, vines and passion fruit combine utility and decoration when they are trained over frameworks to provide shading.

Soft fruits are more difficult to justify in the contained garden because they do little for the aesthetics, and use a lot of space for a small yield. Red currants and gooseberries can be grown as wall plants, but are really better off in a spacious garden. Raspberries need cool roots, fertile soil and plenty of space, but strawberries are far more adaptable and make perfect container subjects. They are attractive plants with pleasing leaves, pretty white flowers and gorgeous red fruits. Their habit of producing trailing runners makes them ideal for hanging over the sides of containers, and they can even be grown in hanging baskets or special planters with pockets in their sides.

With protection from frost, early fruits can be forced, and, provided the right varieties are selected, strawberries can be produced throughout the growing season. The wild strawberry or *fraise des bois is* easy to grow from seed and fruits almost constantly. The fruits, so prized by the French, are scarlet and delicious but so tiny that it takes an afternoon to pick a cupful. The plants themselves are pretty enough to use as edging and easy to propagate.

HERBS

Most herbs make beautiful additions to the contained garden, and, grown in the company of vegetables or ornamentals or both, they contribute enormously. There is not an herb which refuses to grow in a container but a few, notably angelica, lovage, sweet cicely, comfrey and fennel, grow too large for small gardens.

Herbs fall into two general categories: (a) those essential for good, basic cookery, and (b) those of limited culinary use but with certain medicinal properties. Sage fits the former category and feverfew the latter. As far as culture goes, herbs can be treated in the following three groups.

Herbaceous annuals and biennials The most common representatives are parsley, basil and cilantro. Like all annuals and biennials, they need resowing each year. Basil is tender and needs to be raised in a frost-free environment. There are a dozen or more different kinds. Parsley needs a low soil temperature to germinate, and will go to seed and need resowing. Cilantro is worth sowing every month during the growing season to be sure of a steady supply of young leaves. The seed (coriander), which is harvested dry, has a completely different taste from the foliage. All three herbs enjoy good, moist soil.

Herbaceous perennials Tarragon, marjoram and mint are the stars of this group. Mint is highly invasive and needs containing but prefers moist soil. There are several varieties,

ABOVE *Lavender and golden sage are examples of useful culinary herbs which look lovely set alongside ornamental plants.*

ABOVE RIGHT *A container crowded with hyssop and various mints makes an aromatic feature.*

including gold-variegated orange mint, white-variegated apple mint, spearmint and peppermint. The prostrate mint *Mentha pulegium,* also known as pennyroyal, makes an aromatic mat. Marjoram and tarragon are more drought-tolerant than mint. Marjoram is equally pretty in its gold-leaf form, *Origanum vulgare* "Aureum." All three herbs are easy to propagate by division.

Chives are as easy to grow and stay small with fine purple flowers in early summer. Lovage, sweet cicely and angelica, fine for cooking though they undoubtedly are, need plenty of space: angelica, for example, reaches 6 feet or more before it develops a big enough rootstock to flower.

Shrubs and subshrubs Sage, rosemary and thyme are typical examples. All are happy in hot, dry conditions, and will do well in containers in full sun. Thyme can be divided like a perennial, but they all root easily from cuttings. All have interesting garden forms.

Other herbs which may be of less value in the kitchen still make charming container sub-jects, and are well worth growing. Any of the huge host of scented-leaf pelargoniums (geraniums) are desirable, as is lemon verbena, *Aloysia triphylla*, even though it is inclined to grow spindly. Hyssop, whose deep blue flowers are attractive to bees, likes containers, and lavender is useful anywhere. The neatest and strongest colored lavender is *Lavandula angustifolia* "Hidcote" but French lavender, *Lavandula stoechas*, has an interesting smell, reminiscent of eucalyptus, and lovely violet-mauve flowers tipped with "donkey ears."

The joy of herbs is that almost without exception they combine usefulness with beauty and fragrance. They are, therefore, perfect subjects in almost any garden setting, be it formal or informal, patio, balcony or roof.

CONTAINERS
IN THE
GARDEN

*F*rom the humblest suburban backyard to the vast acreage of an estate or palace, pots and planters make a valuable contribution to conventional gardening. They have been employed in gardens laid out in the grand style for centuries, and in modern private gardens, containers are as important as they were in those stately acres of the past.

Terraces, patios, and even swimming pools are barren places without tubs or pots of flowers, or at least some fragrant greenery. Containers are also important as arresting features chosen to take the eye to some point of focus within the garden design or, in a more low-key way, incorporated into a flower bed. And conservatories, which seem set to become as much *à la mode* as they were in the 1860s, now provide a whole new range of opportunities for modern container gardening.

In this chapter I look at the role containers can play in garden design and at their use in overcoming special planting problems or for specific functions. Bonsai, stunted container plants grown by the Japanese for outdoor use, are also covered on pages 108–109.

LEFT *Containers make good focal points in the garden and raise the level of the plants. Here, planting has been designed to give the impression of an abundance of daisies spilling over onto the ground, resulting in a charming, informal effect.*

MAKING THE MOST OF CONTAINERS

Even in spacious, conventional gardens, containers can provide a vital extra dimension. They can increase height, bringing the rose to nose level, as it were, and they can add elegance with their shapes, making a single, central feature or assembled in groups. As in the fully containerized garden, successful container gardening is a matter of planning, choosing the right container and coming up with an imaginative planting which complements the container and the site.

FLOWER BEDS

Although an interesting garden design is likely to consist of borders, paths, lawn and so forth, there is no need for the borders to be exclusively the domain of plants growing in the ground. There are several sound reasons for incorporating containers into a garden border, either as conspicuous special features or blended into the background.

A large, good-looking tub or pot can be positioned to become the focal point of a border. The planting in this container can then be designed either to complement the rest of the border – perhaps actually including some of the species which grow in the ground around it – or to make an arresting contrast. In a border where foliage and soft color predominates, for example, a brighter color or a deeper shade of flower could be selected for

the container. Conversely, if flowers predominate in the border, a dark evergreen with a distinctive shape will stand out well and would provide winter interest too.

Containers may also be incorporated into a border for the sake of plants which could not otherwise be included. Tender species which are "on loan" from the greenhouse for a while, or perhaps those which dislike your soil (page 102), may blend beautifully with their surroundings but still need to continue life in a container. The wonderful foliage plant, *Meliantlus major*, for example, is hopelessly tender in a cold climate, but can be placed outdoors for weeks in the summer, producing a marvelous crop of glaucous foliage resembling oversized salad burnet, and making a breathtaking contrast with pink or red roses.

Equally, there may be plants in the greenhouse which you want to lend to the border because they have flowers or foliage of just the right color to complete some carefully planned association, or because they are only worth looking at in flower and would waste space at other times.

However you choose to use containers in your flower beds, it is important to remember that if they are placed directly onto soil, two problems may occur. First, the soil may not give enough support, allowing the container to sink down on one side, tilt or even in time fall over. And second, soil could eventually plug

the drainage holes, especially if ants or worms carry it up into the container. It is therefore essential to stand all containers on a firm, flat base. Bricks are particularly useful here, as is a single flagstone.

VISTA STOPS

"Vista" is really just a fancy word for a view, but to the garden designer it means a long, narrow prospect. Vistas are often associated with trees, so looking down a poplar-lined avenue is one example of a vista. A similar effect can be achieved with two rows of shrubs or double hedges, or by erecting some kind of arbor or framework for climbing plants. Even two buildings so close together that the space between them is little more than a narrow corridor can, with skillful design, be transformed into a vista.

ABOVE *In a predominantly green planting, the pot of pink verbena has provided a cheerful splash of color which will last all summer.*

OPPOSITE LEFT *With a golden cypress to act as background, this alpine sink blends perfectly into its garden setting.*

OPPOSITE RIGHT *A gap in the foliage here is filled with a clay pot of white nicotiana.*

ABOVE *Clipped hedges with dark foliage make an effective backdrop for the focal point – a white, brightly planted Versailles tub.*

OPPOSITE *This elaborate container is complemented by a simple two-color planting of silver* Stachys *and white* Impatiens.

But why create a vista? The quick answer is that it adds interest to the garden. Vistas give an impression of size and space. They "orchestrate" the scenery so that your point of view changes as you wander around. A cunningly planned garden will consist of a series of hedges, screens or barriers which seem to bar your way when seen "head on," but which line the views along tempting paths when you look down their lengths. Change your position in the garden and what was a screen directs you toward another area.

Whether these vistas radiate from a central point or run in criss-cross fashion, they are pointless without some focal point at the end, that is, a "vista stop." Looking down an empty alley is uninteresting because your eye automatically clicks to the end, to see the way ahead, and an empty prospect is always disappointing. If there is something to attract attention, on the other hand, your interest is maintained and even stimulated.

At a central point in the garden, with paths radiating from it, the same stop will have to do for all the vistas when looking from the outsides inward but, when you stand at the center, there should also be something to entice you outward along each path. Obviously the central vista stop will have to be pretty major – the focal point of the whole garden – but every one of the subordinate outer stops should also be so tempting that you find yourself in an agony of indecision about which route to wander down first.

In grand gardens the major stop could be an enormous nude statue, but in the average back garden a large planter could be all the excitement you can take — or need! The container itself should be attractive and distinctive, and its planting designed to set it off rather than to obscure its character. The outer vista stops, in formal gardens, might consist of matching pots or planters, with a similar planting scheme in each. In more informal gardens, there might be a variety of features, including containers at the ends of some paths and just a bright shrub, a little statue or perhaps a small seat at the ends of others.

A final point about vista stops: however they are composed, they must be conspicuous enough to demand attention. Height is important, but color and texture matter too. In gloomy surroundings, a pale limestone urn planted with silver foliage and white flowers will stand out much more than a terracotta pot

OPPOSITE RIGHT *This clipped bay tree can be taken indoors for winter protection. Anemones form the delightful summer underplanting.*

LEFT *For the enthusiastic herbalist with limited space, a tiered rack of pots in baskets is an appealing solution, insuring each plant an adequate supply of light.*

BELOW *The horticultural terracottary set out like a shrine makes an amusing group which could easily be moved elsewhere, if required.*

planted with deep red geraniums, but in a well-lit spot orange or red will be more conspicuous, and pale pinks or lilacs might look rather washed out.

FILLERS

Small pot plants are as much part of the outdoor garden scene as in the house. A shelf, ledge, low wall or table outside is just as suitable a place for a small container as is an indoor windowsill. There are three main differences between interior and exterior "houseplants."

Light There is almost always more light outdoors, and therefore the choice of plants which can be grown is wider.

Water Since the evaporation rate in summer is always much higher outdoors than it is in the house, plants in small pots outside will need watering more frequently, particularly those that are nearly pot-bound. For instance, a pelargonium (geranium), 18 inches high, in full bloom and growing in a 5–7-inch pot, could need watering as often as three times a day in hot, dry weather. With a large number of small containers outdoors, the watering chore in summer could become very time-consuming and tedious.

Wind Small pots do not just blow over, they roll about until the pot is broken and the plant's leaves are all mangled. Small pots outdoors must therefore be placed in a sheltered spot, or tied down or weighted. Very small plants, or subjects with low centers of gravity or little wind-resistance, are less susceptible to wind damage, so cactus plants, for example, or anything with a prostrate habit, are less likely to be damaged.

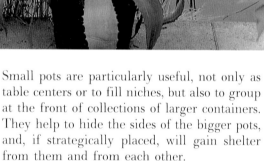

Small pots are particularly useful, not only as table centers or to fill niches, but also to group at the front of collections of larger containers. They help to hide the sides of the bigger pots, and, if strategically placed, will gain shelter from them and from each other.

WATER FEATURES

Water is important because it gives depth to any garden design – by reflecting the sky, it adds more light to the space and by reflecting its immediate surroundings, it contributes a valuable extra dimension. Except when reflecting the revolting blue paint which seems to be the norm for most swimming pools, water is restful and does soothing things to the psyche. Although gazing into a limpid pool might seem to have the same boredom quotient as watching paint dry, it can distract troubled souls for hours, especially when

ABOVE LEFT *Containers, with tender plants, are used here to embellish a water feature.*

ABOVE *This woodland habitat makes a shaded terrace which is an ideal site for containerized ferns and other shade lovers.*

OPPOSITE *Classical design is enhanced here by using a severely clipped potted tree.*

there are beautiful plants, fish, frogs or even invertebrate wiggly things to watch.

Containers seem to belong naturally with water margins. A formal pond, whether straight-sided or circular, tends to look stark or severe unless it is embellished with containers of some sort. Where there is no soil next to the pool – it may be surrounded by paving, for instance – containers enable plants to be placed near the water's edge so that

vegetation can be reflected in its surface. Pots of plants also help to set off other structures, such as seats, statues or gazebos, all of which can be sited so that they reflect in the water.

Informal ponds or lakes can look equally good with an urn or two nearby. On a big lake, a landing stage or jetty can become a little formal area, decorated with standing pots. Even with small, informal ponds set aside purely for wildlife, a carefully chosen and planted container or two will add to the attraction without compromising the habitat or your design.

TERRACES AND PATIOS

I may as well admit straight away that I hate the word "patio." It seems to conjure up an image of colored concrete paving slabs, a set of gaudy furniture and access to the house through enormous sliding glass structures which leak when it rains and are drafty in winter. Such a place might be littered with plastic Georgian urns containing French marigolds and scarlet salvias or even planters crammed with plastic flowers.

A "terrace," on the other hand, has upper-class pretensions – the sort of place where Noël Coward might have wafted, wearing a silk bathrobe, holding a cup of breakfast coffee and looking with disdain at his hostess's geraniums. It would, inevitably, be paved with genuine stone flags and furnished with, perhaps, an antique lead tank, with a dolphin design in bas-relief. There might be some antique terracotta pots, each in conventional shape and decorated with garlands of clay roses and foliage. Seats would be few and far between, made uncomfortably of hardwood in a chinoiserie or Indian design. The pots might hold geraniums or tulips, but planting would be severe, rather than lavish, and colors would be strictly regulated.

Both images are extreme, of course, and it would be facetious to go on in this vein. Indeed, you may be bristling with fury at my supposed condescension, in which case remember my comments in the chapter on design – it is important to grow what you like and not what fashion or someone else's taste dictates. What follows are simply suggestions based on my experiences and prejudices.

In spite of my earlier strictures, modern patios need not be limited to muted colors. Going for a rich variety of foliage – not just leaf color but texture and leaf shapes as well – and choosing distinctive plants will result in a far more pleasing display. Being original in your selection of plants pays off every time.

Hostas, for example, make lovely container subjects for patios, their foliage arching over the sides of the pots. Several grasses, especially *Hakonechloa macra* "Aureola," group well with hostas and other flowering plants, particularly when grown in low containers.

There is never any need, with modern patio designs, to be conventional as far as containers are concerned. Indeed, it is far better to choose exactly the right receptacle for the plant. Wide, shallow dishes, even if they are a yard in diameter, suit low, spreading plants; tall containers, perhaps even old chimney pots, are fine for trailing plants, and clusters of small pots, dotted around seemingly at random, help to enrich the display.

ABOVE *Summer additions to a formal area include pots of petunias, which provide a boost of color and interest. Note only one color has been used in each container.*

RIGHT *A sitting area, between border and pool, is decorated for summer with a clipped bay and potted petunia. The white container may match the metal furniture, but the terracotta is more sympathetic.*

OPPOSITE *With frost-hardy subjects, containers make excellent winter features, and help to maintain design structure. In summer small pots of flowering plants used as fillers would strike a lighter note.*

With period houses, there is less scope for the off-beat in containers. Ultra-modern planters, unless carefully selected, will look out of place, and old-style pots tend to be fairly conventional in shape and decoration. But as for planting, the choice is as wide as you like. The colors of some modern hybrid roses or dahlias may be a little too powerful for the antique atmosphere. You need to take into account the colors of the building materials of the house and try to harmonize with them, but, even allowing for those constraints, the choice that remains is inexhaustible.

Several pelargonium (geranium) species are particularly good near old houses because of their more subtle coloration, and they have the added benefit of fragrant foliage. Certain plants seem "right" against a backdrop of old brick, whereas others go better with stone. Heliotrope is so somber a purple and has such rich scent that it belongs almost anywhere with almost any scheme. All the silver-leaved plants, especially helichrysums, *Senecio bicolor* subsp. *cineraria* (syn. *S. maritimus*), *Senecio leuchostachys*, artemisias and lavenders, are of immense value, either as background planting or as lovely features on their own.

Fuchsias, especially those with soft colors, are useful because they flower for so long and therefore make valuable background planting. The older, smaller-flowered fuchsia varieties frequently bloom more profusely, and are much easier to blend into a general planting scheme than some of the huge-flowered modern hybrids.

KITCHEN GARDENS

A prettily designed potager will have lots of pots standing about with colorful herbs and vegetables growing in them. From the purely practical point of view, these may need too much attention to be worth the trouble, but, before you dismiss the notion, remember that they do provide a useful means of growing tender food plants outdoors.

Tomatoes, sweet bell peppers, eggplants and chilies can be started off under glass

before the frost-free period has begun, and then wheeled out as soon as it is safe. Growing them that way enables you to steal a march on the climate by having mature plants earlier than if they had been planted directly into the ground. In cold, sluggish growing conditions this is a distinct advantage. Tender herbs, especially basil, can be grown in the same way, sowing the seed in late winter under glass and moving the containers outdoors in late spring when the risk of frost has completely passed.

If you want to introduce ornamental planting into the kitchen garden, one way of

having plenty of color without competing too strongly with the vegetables would be to fill planters with colorful annuals or bedding plants and to group them among the vegetables. Whitefly hate French marigolds, so they could have a useful deterrent effect, although, to work properly, they need to have their roots in contact with susceptible plants, particularly tomatoes and sweet bell peppers (page 138).

The suitability of strawberries as container plants has already been covered on page 86, but it is worth remembering that they make decorative and effective container plants anywhere in the garden.

TOP *The containers holding these tomatoes are purely functional, enabling the plants to grow in special compost. Note the canary creeper added purely for decoration.*

ABOVE *A narrow border has been extended by placing three pots at its end. Trailing helichrysum and petunias bring a lightness which complements the darker greens.*

ABOVE LEFT *This well-ordered potager is both pleasing and productive. The urn adds style to the plan, but it pays its rent by making a home for a squash plant.*

SOLVING SPECIAL PROBLEMS

Apart from the obvious aesthetic advantages of using containers in the garden, there are a number of sound, practical reasons for their use. Indeed, containers were almost certainly first used in horticulture for reasons of cultivation rather than decoration. The raised beds of medieval medicinal gardens, where soil which had been enriched with dung was retained by wooden planking, were, in effect, special containers. Each bed could be treated differently so that the special needs of a particular group of plants could be catered to without adversely influencing the others.

One of the most frustrating aspects of modern gardening is that, in spite of all our technology, we are relatively powerless to change the chemical nature of our soil. Of course, we can improve texture with composts and mulches, and step up fertility with manures and fertilizers; we can even make minor adjustments to acidity with lime or with flowers of sulphur (page 123). But, in spite of everything we do at the surface, plant roots tend to run deep, and, if the subsoil does not suit them, they will sicken and die. With container gardening that problem can often be circumvented by supplying an appropriate soil type wherever it is required.

CALCIFUGES

A calcifuge is a plant which cannot thrive in alkaline or limy soil. (Chapter and verse on acidity, lime and pH are given on page 123 — my object here is to explain the implications.) People often bemoan their misfortunes if their land is alkaline, but, since there are tens of thousands of fine plants which grow vigorously in limy soil, it is difficult to understand why. The answer has to do partly with horticultural snobbery and partly because so many of the world's most handsome plants occur in naturally acidic soil.

Rhododendrons, for example, insist on acid soil. To my mind many of them are detestable with their lugubrious dark foliage, unnaturally bright flowers and toxic nectar, but they seem to be at the top of most people's

"wants" list. Many species of lilies also need acid soil; so do gorgeous blue Himalayan poppies, camellias, many species of heather and such woodland and mountain beauties as trilliums and fall gentians. There are also thousands of marginal species which, though happy in neutral soil, will not take lime: pieris species, fothergilla, smilacina, nerine and so on. If your garden soil is strongly alkaline, how do you grow any of these treasures? For some, the simple answer is to use containers.

Containers permit the use of different composts so that a variety of plants quite alien to the local habitat can be grown. Thus, even if your garden is on thin soil overlying chalk, it will still be possible for you to enjoy pots of *Lilium speciosum* in summer and to pick camellia blossoms in early spring. It sounds quite easy and straightforward, but there are some important points to be considered.

Compatibility Many calcifuges, especially the thousands introduced to the West from the Himalayas, relish a cool, moist climate besides needing acid soil. Acid soil alone, for example, will not be enough to allow petiolarid primulas such as *Primula whitei* or the exquisite pink-flowered shortias to survive if they are kept in a hot, dry environment.

ABOVE *Calcifuges like this azalea will thrive in a lime-free container.*

OPPOSITE A Cyclamen persicum *is ideal in a frost-free area for winter color and scent.*

Seepage Although drainage is essential, direct contact with outside soil can cause problems. A calcifuge in a tub will, as its root system matures and fills the compost, send rootlets into the natural soil below the container. With apparently suicidal instincts, the plant then absorbs too many calcium ions and develops chlorosis – paling of the leaves – and may eventually die. Standing the container on a brick base can help.

Water In limestone areas, tap water is usually "hard," which means alkaline. Therefore, if calcifuges are watered with tap water for any length of time, the compost in the container will become alkaline, and the plant will languish. Calcifuges must be watered with rainwater. (See page 123 for decontamination treatment for small quantities of limy soil.)

LIME LOVERS

Some gardeners have the opposite problem soil which is naturally too acid to sustain lime-loving plants. Most vegetables, especially brassicas, beets, peas and beans, prefer limy soil. Pinks and carnations, delphiniums and a large number of alpines will only thrive in alkaline soil, and all clematis species prefer it. Therefore, if the natural material is sharp acid sand or peaty loam, it may be necessary to consider containers with limy composts for a few subjects.

DIFFICULT ASPECTS

Although this has already been mentioned several times elsewhere in the book, it is worth emphasizing here that containers do have certain advantages over soil where planting conditions are far from ideal, especially in an exposed position. In a particularly exposed spot, for example, it may be almost impossible to get a windbreak established because conditions are so harsh. Placing already established plants in containers to windward may do the trick by affording shelter to the young plants in the ground so that they can become stronger and grow to make the permanent shelter more quickly. You may have to accept that the containerized shelter is expendable, if it is slowly ruined while it affords shelter to the young permanent plants, but this is still a worthwhile exercise.

An alternative approach, if the site is particularly hostile, is to treat the container plants as disposable from the outset. As they are spoiled, simply replace them with new purchases or with newly grown plants. However, in poorly lit areas, if a rotation of plants is organized so that none stays in the gloom for longer than a couple of weeks with a similar "recovery" period in full light, it is possible to recycle the same plants many times without destroying them.

COVERS AND CLOCHES

If you think of cloches and covers as "upside-down containers," you will not balk at their inclusion here. Like containers, they create their own mini-environment, and this ability can help solve particular cultivation problems. The use of cloches with vegetables is well known, but few gardeners appreciate the potential use of cloches for ornamentals.

ABOVE *The handles on this container make it easy to move the ficus plant about, giving it short spells in a hostile environment followed by periods of rehabilitation.*

OPPOSITE TOP *In a gloomy spot, pale shades are often more effective than bright colors. Here, pale cream variegated ivy and white flowers work together perfectly.*

OPPOSITE BOTTOM *Young plants and tender species often benefit from temporary protection, provided here by inverted jars, from cold as well as from excessive wet.*

Literally meaning "bell" in French, the original cloches were really nothing more than bell jars that were placed over young plants for protection. Used in the garden with containers, cloches and covers are useful for the following three reasons.

Protection from excessive rainfall A cloche or cover can be used to keep the worst of the wet weather off certain plants. Petiolarid primulas may abhor dry heat but they can also rot in a wet winter. Popping a cloche over them in the wettest periods can snatch success from the jaws of botrytis. Certain silver-foliage plants, though they may be perfectly frost hardy, succumb to soggy winter weather and can also benefit from a short-term cover.

Humidity This may seem to be in contradiction of the first point, but in certain conditions a cloche will insure high relative humidity, especially when the compost is kept damp at all times. Insectivorous plants such as sundews (*Drosera* spp.), pitcher plants (*Sarracenia* spp.) and Venus's flytrap (*Dionaea muscipula*) all benefit from the humidity provided by a cloche. They also need to grow in pure moss or mosspeat, preferably sphagnum, and to be waterlogged.

Warmth A cloche provides warmth in two ways: first, by behaving like a little greenhouse, its interior warms up much more in sunlight than does the air outside; second, since it keeps rain off, it warms and dries the soil. Both factors speed up plant growth, producing, for example, precocious blooms, early strawberries or quick lettuces.

One huge drawback about cloches and covers is that they are seldom a pretty sight. Occasionally, you can find attractive antique specimens, such as four-sided cloches, with glazing bars and a little handle at the top. Bell jars and rounded cloches also sometimes turn up, and lovely they are. Old forcing pots intended for rhubarb or seakale are equally useful and decorative, besides their "romantic" associations with old kitchen gardens and the days when trusty retainers worked a 100-hour week for a handful of loose change. But the modern contraptions of plastic, wire and galvanized metal are unlikely to do much for the aesthetic quality of the garden.

There is no reason why decorative cloches, bells or forcing pots should not be manufactured today. They would be easy enough to produce, but so far the demand has not been there. Perhaps, now that some gardeners are having a love affair with nineteenth-century style, a manufacturer somewhere will come up with the product.

ABOVE *These tiny cloches have been placed to protect the plants from extremes of temperature. Although these are elegant examples, jam jars, bases of plastic bottles or even polyetheline bags are just as effective for keeping delicate plants warm and shielding them from excessive rain.*

OPPOSITE *Every plantsman's garden needs a number of translucent devices to provide temporary protection for plants for a number of reasons: to hasten seed germination, to keep alpines dry during wet seasons and to protect winter flowers from weather damage. This cloche is in the traditional shape.*

BONSAI

Bonsai is an ancient form of container grow-ing which originated in China, where it is known as *pen-jing*, and was adopted and altered by the Japanese. Like so much Japan-ese garden culture, it consists of contriving a natural appearance by unnatural treatment. The term "bonsai" means "tray-planted," and it is used to describe woody plants which have been grown to simulate maturity or great age even though they have been restricted to being no more than 2 feet tall.

Contrary to common belief in the West, bonsai trees are not traditionally houseplants. In Japan they are kept outdoors and only brought in for special display, and for no more than a few days at a time. For outdoor use, they are superb and, as long as the winters are not too harsh, they should survive without

extra protection. However, where winter frosts are severe, it may pay to place them in a cold frame or unheated greenhouse, even if merely to protect the ceramic dishes in which the trees are planted.

Bonsai trees can be used in exactly the same way as any other small container plant, whether on tables or standing on the ground, and can make a valuable contribution to any kind of conventional garden. However, they are trained to be viewed only from one side, something which always must be borne in mind when incorporating them into your gar-den plan.

There are several distinct styles of bonsai, but the general idea is to imitate the looks of a tree which has been knocked about by the weather, and gnarled and twisted with age.

The different shapes have special Japanese names: *chokkan,* for example, refers to a stately, upright tree; *shakan* means a tree with a slanting trunk; and *kengai* refers to a tree which overhangs its tray in the way that a wild tree would hang over a cliff. Singly planted bonsai trees are called *ippon-ue,* groups are known as *yoseue,* and a tree with its roots embedded in and growing over a lump of pumice is called *ishizuke.*

Bonsai trees are long-lived and become extremely valuable as they age. In Japan they are family heirlooms, and in the West mind-boggling prices can be paid for them. If you wish to buy mature plants, be ready to spend a considerable sum, but, if you want to grow your own, the investment will be in time rather than money.

There is a wide choice of plants which will allow themselves to be abused in this way. Traditionally, the Japanese have used junipers, *Cryptomeria japonica, Acer palmatum, Chaenomeles japonica,* hawthorn species and many others. *Metasequoia glyptostroboides* also lends itself to bonsai, as do several species of cherry and the beautiful, scented Japanese apricot, *Prunus mume.*

BONSAI-LIKE PLANTS

Certain plants behave almost as though they were bonsai without needing any special attention. These look more natural, and are mostly easy to grow.

Japanese holly, *Ilex crenata,* has tiny, glossy evergreen leaves and little black or white berries. In a container it will stay small and stubby for decades.

Certain willows, particularly *Salix boydii* and *Salix helvetica,* are small and neat, making useful container subjects, the latter being one of the few silver-foliage plants which loves cool, moist shade. *Salix arbuscula* can be encouraged to grow up on short trunks and then trail down elegantly, and although *Salix repens* has lax, untidy stems, it is worth growing for its needlepoint catkins, which look like tiny silver lights.

ABOVE *A Bonsai pine tree grows in a handsome dish. This shape has been achieved by judicious pruning and training with special wires. The roots have to be pruned ideally each year, and every third year at least, to preserve the dwarf stature, yet feeding is important if the tree is to thrive. The position of the tree in the container is always determined by the growing style adopted.*

OPPOSITE *Bonsai trees make delightful container subjects for standing outdoors on tables or ledges. It takes many years of careful culture for a specimen as fine as this cypress to develop its mature looks. Note the gnarled and twisted trunk, the well-spaced branches and the size of the foliage, all in perfect proportion with the scale of the tree.*

CONSERVATORIES

The conservatory plays an important part in a garden where containers are used. It can serve as elegant nursemaid to your tenderest container shrubs during the winter months, and, by extension, it can also help you bridge the gap between outside and inside. Sitting at the open doors when the weather is bright but not exactly hot is one of the joys of spring or fall, or even a mild day in winter.

This feeling of continuity with the garden can be reinforced by having containerized plants both inside and out. A little terrace outside the main doors could accommodate citrus trees in tubs, or neatly clipped myrtles or bays, which would spend all summer outside but come in for winter. The linking theme could be continued with tender flowering plants in urns or pots, or by placing specimen plants, seemingly at random, both inside and out.

The problem with overwintering all the tender containerized shrubs in a conservatory is that there may not be room left for winter sitting. The alternative is to erect a greenhouse specifically for overwintering (page 137).

Although greenhouses had been in use since the seventeenth century, the conservatory was not developed until the nineteenth century. Joseph Paxton built the giant one at Chatsworth House in Derbyshire, England, and designed the Crystal Palace for the Great Exhibition of 1851. But in fact, the iron glazing-bar – a structure strong enough to support considerable weight, light enough to be used in extensive roofworks and thin enough to allow the roofing to consist mainly of glass, and therefore let in plenty of daylight – was the invention of a gardening genius of the earlier 1800s, John Claudius Loudon.

RIGHT TOP *The passion flower,* Passiflora caerulea, *is a fine conservatory climber.*

RIGHT BOTTOM *This fine yellow abutilon shades a conservatory and provides color.*

OPPOSITE *Under glass, pelargoniums can be allowed to run wild with splendid results.*

The conservatory was perfect for the nineteenth-century obsession with collecting exotic curiosities. Its popularity has waxed and waned over the last 150 years, but lately the concept has found great favor in some circles once more. With the advent of bendable plastics and light alloy fittings, a rush of nineteenth-century imitations has flooded the market. Each year their prices break new records as the quantity of fancy embellishments increases, but few prefabricated conservatories on today's market are designed for the comfort of the plants. Inadequate ventilation is their worst deficiency, with too few openable roof lights and sometimes no opening side windows at all.

If a conservatory is to be used for plants, it should have the following features.

Good ventilation There should be a continuous line of roof vents, preferably automatically operated, so that excessive temperatures are avoided without having to shade the glass. Ventilators near the ground should be designed so that air can circulate freely without creating cold drafts.

ABOVE *Amaryllis* (Hippeastrum aulicum) *can be raised in a greenhouse, and brought into the conservatory when blooming has begun.*

OPPOSITE *A conservatory can be laid out as an indoor garden with tempting pathways.*

Generous outside doors Wide and preferably double doors are essential. These should be large enough to enable bulky plants in awkward tubs to be maneuvered in and out without damage or injury – either to the plants or the gardener.

Waterproof fittings Priceless carpets, smart wall hangings and indoor electrical outlets are quite useless in a proper conservatory because you need to be able to hose the entire area down from time to time.

Provided the basic needs of the plant can be met without compromising its appeal as a place in which to sit, a conservatory can become the focal point of a garden, enjoyable in all weathers and attractive both inside and out.

SEASONAL EFFECTS

In every garden there are certain times of year when things are a little dull. If the emphasis is on shrubs, for example, late winter or high summer can be colorless. Few flower after midsummer, and by the end of winter even the loveliest evergreens begin to grow boring. Equally, English-style herbaceous borders can be dreary expanses of dead vegetation throughout winter, or, if trimmed up in the fall, barren wastelands.

One way to overcome these dead spots is to use containers on a temporary basis. But, as with all your garden planning, be realistic in your expectations: different seasons need different approaches, and some times of year are easier to liven than others.

SPRING

The most obvious stopgap is provided by bulbs, which can be purchased almost in flower or grown on from dry bulbs. They can be transplanted with relative ease at almost any stage of growth, and, when planted, need very little further attention. This means that if the site where they are to flower is not ready until winter's end – perhaps because something else is growing there – they can be grown on elsewhere, and moved when the site is ready.

OPPOSITE *A problem spot, such as the dark base of this tree, can be highlighted with temporary containers. These pelargoniums would not thrive here forever, but will give several weeks of enjoyment before they fade.*

BELOW *Nothing beats bulbs for a bright spring effect, created here with species of tulips and alliums. Narcissi, crocuses or hyacinths would be equally cheerful.*

Hyacinths and dwarf tulips are the most amenable to this *ad hoc* treatment, and can be started into growth in the fall in seed trays – or in decorative containers – under a layer of moist peat. When they are needed, simply transplant them or move the containers.

Although bulbs last for many years planted deeply in containers, if a dense mass of bloom is wanted, a different approach is needed. Daffodils and tulips can be planted so densely that the bulbs are almost touching. The resulting exuberant display will hardly look natural but there will be a good splash of color. If bulbs are being grown for cutting, they can be planted equally densely. But beware: in subsequent years, disease would be the inevitable result of such overcrowding, so bulbs grown densely should be treated as annuals and discarded or planted elsewhere in the garden after flowering.

Spring bedding plants, as long as they have always been outdoors, can withstand transplanting surprisingly late. Wallflowers take exception, and usually die if they are not planted out by late fall, but primroses, forget-me-nots and above all pansies and violas move happily at almost any time, even when they have begun flowering.

SUMMER

Throughout this book the emphasis has been on summer displays, and ideas for well composed containers occur on almost every page, but there is one way in which the season can be heightened further, perhaps for a special occasion. At any flower show, the most attractive exhibits are usually the nurserymen's trade displays, where potted flowering plants are arranged to look their best for a few days. By skillful use of backing material, moss and graded pot sizes, the containers can all be concealed to create a very natural effect. This kind of exhibit, on a smaller scale, could make a stylish centerpiece for a party or function in the garden, and will last for a surprisingly long time, especially if plants which begin to show stress are removed or replaced.

OPPOSITE Viburnum tinus *has evergreen foliage and long-lasting winter flowers.*

BELOW *The California bluebell,* Phacelia campanularia, *makes a delightful centerpiece.*

WINTER

Very little can be done, on a temporary basis, about improving winter effects except to buy flowering or seasonal plants and hope that they will survive outdoors for a while. I have seen city window boxes, in the depths of winter, planted up with such tender subjects as cinerarias, *Solanum capsicastrum* and maiden-hair fern. With the local micro-climate, these manage to get by for a few weeks before succumbing, but finding constant replacements can be an expensive business. It is probably better, and certainly cheaper, to rely on sound year-round planning and to have winter-flowering plants in the general planting scheme, either in containers or in the ground.

Winter is the season which exposes all your planning errors. If a garden walk on the year's shortest day is not only a pleasurable and interesting experience but also yields a bunch of something to put into a vase indoors, you will have earned your sense of triumph. Containers are not the only way to achieve this, but the chances are your winter walk would have been duller without them.

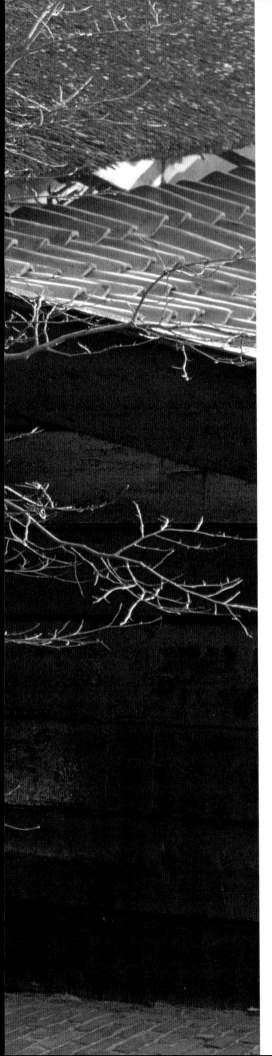

GARDENING
TECHNIQUES

*T*here is no deep mystery about container culture. No abstruse technical training is required, but it does help to understand the basic needs of green plants. To survive, they must have water, air, light and nutrients. To thrive, they must enjoy protection from climatic extremes and from diseases. Such needs are fundamental but there is more. To look their best, different plants merit special treatment: climbers need training and support, some shrubs require pruning in certain ways to flower really well, hedges or topiary plants need regular clipping, perennials must be cut back, and annuals need replanting each season.

Keeping plants alive requires minimal skill. Growing them really well calls for a greater technical input, but much of the knowhow is instinctive, particularly if you have a fondness for growing things. Call it "green fingers" or "green thumb" if you like, but what it amounts to is good husbandry – an inborn quality but one which is enhanced by experience. You may not have developed your own skills yet, but you certainly have a love of plants. If you had not, you would not have read this far!

This chapter outlines some of the practical aspects of container gardening. For easy reference, topics are arranged under headings.

LEFT *Container-grown trees and shrubs need regular pruning to keep their shape.*

THE CONTAINER

Containers are not natural. Few plants would choose to establish themselves in tubs or pots, where they depend on artificial aids to survive, so to insure the best results, careful thought is needed about the types of container to be used.

The aim must always be to match the container to the chosen plant's particular requirements, that is, to make the environment as natural as possible. The size of container is obviously important here, but you must also bear in mind the effects of temperature on your containers, whether hot or cold. Only after these considerations have been resolved can you indulge personal tastes as far as shapes and styles of planters are concerned.

CONTAINER SIZE

The larger the container, the happier its occupants will be. There are several reasons for this.
● In a garden or natural environment, plants spread their root systems a surprisingly long way, but in a container it is seldom possible for them to reach their maximum rootrun. Generally, this poses no problem as long as adequate water and nutrition are always available, but a badly cramped root system cannot function properly at all. Even with small plants, a generous rootrun will always make for a much sturdier specimen: well-developed roots make a secure anchorage so wind damage is minimized.
● Large containers are heavier, and therefore less likely to blow over.
● Large containers retain moisture for longer, and suffer smaller temperature changes than small ones.
● Large containers offer more scope for mixed plantings.

TEMPERATURE

Containers can be damaged by frost action. Unlike practically everything else, water expands as the temperature drops from 32°F to 25°F. This change in structure can affect containers in two ways. First, as the moisture soaked into porous material expands to form ice, it causes fragments to break off. Second, the expanding moisture content of compost in frosty conditions can create stress fractures in the walls of some planters. Conventional plant pots with tapering sides are less likely to crack than waisted containers, or those which are narrow at the top. When compost freezes in a tapered pot, the whole bulk tends to slip upward, easing the pressure on the sides of the container.

In addition to container damage, plants too may suffer in frosty weather. Many plants, even those which are quite hardy, will not tolerate frozen roots. In the ground, roots would grow deep enough to stay clear of the frost, but the contents of containers often freeze right through unless insulated. Some species of holly, rhododendron and clematis are especially susceptible to this problem.

The solution, for cold areas, is to select frost-proof containers and plants which are root-hardy, to provide winter protection, or to bring containers indoors for the duration of winter. (See page 137 for suggestions on overwintering.)

Extreme heat is also stressful to plants. Roots operate best at relatively low, steady temperatures, and heat-absorbent containers placed in direct sun tend to cook their contents. Black containers, especially black metal or plastic ones, are particularly susceptible to heat, but white timber or thick stone buffers it, and trailing plants hanging over the sides provide extra shade. Positioning helps too. Heat-lovers such as echeverias placed on the sunny side of a container group could protect more delicate plants with their shade.

LEFT *Containers must suit their occupants. This urn is just right for the hydrangea now, but by next year the plant will be grown to twice the size and something larger will be needed.*

RIGHT *The variety of container styles is almost infinite. Terracotta weathers nicely, but suffers in frost. Small pots like these are ideal for grouping, but dry out quickly and could freeze through in winter.*

BELOW *Wooden half-barrels make inexpensive containers for shrubs like this rose or for large perennials. Their shape makes them stable and roomy enough to allow a generous rootrun. Wood is a poor conductor of heat, insuring cooler compost in hot weather.*

THE SOIL

Healthy soil is crucial. Natural soil is a mixture of minerals and organic matter with a granular structure which allows it to retain air and moisture. The particles themselves are surrounded with a film of water, and air fills the spaces between them. Soil is teeming with life. There are earthworms, nematodes, fungi, bacteria, protozoa, insects and a lot more besides.

Plant roots, with the aid of tiny hairs, probe the soil to absorb water, along with dissolved mineral salts. If dry, the root hairs perish, but equally, if the tiny spaces between soil particles are saturated with water, so that there is no space for air, the root hairs also perish. Thus, drainage is important to allow surplus water to run away through the soil (pages 124-125).

In containers, some of the natural characteristics of soil are inevitably lost, but unless it can "breathe" – that is, hold air and moisture within its structure – and can provide all the mineral elements needed by the plants, it will not support them. Most containers are filled with prepared soil mixes, known as "composts," but whatever kinds are used, they must meet those two requirements.

TYPES OF COMPOST

There are two distinct types of compost, "soilless" and "loam-based," but within each type are hundreds of different formulae. The term "soilless" is a little

misleading, but for our purpose it means any compost based on organic matter, usually peat derived from sphagnum moss or sedge, to which essential nutrients have been added.

A good loam-based potting compost consists, by volume, of seven parts loam, three parts moss peat and two parts sand, plus added lime, potassium, nitrogen and phosphorus. All growing media, whether loam-based or soilless, should be of the optimum physical structure for strong root development, contain sufficient nutrients for healthy plant development, and be free of all harmful organisms .

Soilless composts have . the following advantages.
● They are much lighter, making them easier to handle, less weighty in roof

gardens and balconies, and less expensive too.
● Being more bulky and less dense than loam, they retain their structure, are easy to plant, and more pleasant on the hands.
● They are better for lime-hating plants because they are naturally acidic. (It is important to check that no lime has been added if you are preparing containers for such plants.)

But there are also some disadvantages .
● Containers filled with soilless compost are lighter, and therefore more liable to be blown over by the wind.
● Soilless compost is fairly water retentive, but, when it has dried out, it *repels* water, and is therefore often difficult to remoisten.
● Soilless compost is less tolerant of misapplication of fertilizer. Loam tends to

ABOVE *Given moist, gritty soil, flat pans of alpine* Rhodohypoxis baurii *will multiply freely.*

OPPOSITE *In a cool green ensemble, the spectacular* Eucomis *is perfect for planting in free-draining compost in full sun.*

create buffers, so that any nutrient deficiencies or surpluses are less apparent in the plants.

ACQUIRING THE RIGHT COMPOST

If you have access to good loam and prefer to know exactly what is going into your compost, it is probably better to mix your own, I tend to vary my particular recipe according to what ingredients are available, but, generally, my mixes contain roughly one third each, by volume, of plain garden soil, moss peat (from sphagnum) and coarse sand. For indoor pots, or raising seeds, I use a sterile compost purchased in large bags, but for large outdoor containers I have not yet found soil sterilization to be necessary.

Ready-made compost contains plantfood and lime, but in my mixes I simply add a slow-release compound fertilizer at the level recommended by the manufacturer. I live in a limy area, so my natural soil is already alkaline and needs no additional lime.

For those who have too little space or lack the inclination to mix their own, the market abounds with ready-made potting composts. It is beyond the scope of this book to review them all, but often the best way to find out how well a product performs is to try it.

In some gardens, plants are grown in containers because they will not thrive in the local garden soil. Typical of these would be calcifuges such as azaleas or rhododendrons growing in a limestone area. It is essential, in these cases, to use ericaceous or lime-free

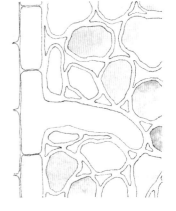

RIGHT Soil is living material, and to support plant life, it must have a healthy structure. Every particle should be coated with a film of moisture, but there must be air spaces between them to allow the root hairs to "breathe" as they absorb moisture and dissolved minerals. Correct watering and efficient drainage will insure the right conditions.

composts, and also to remember to water the plants only with rainwater. (Water which has been softened by a domestic water softener is too saline and will harm most plants.)

ACID OR ALKALINE?

In alkaline soil, lime-hating plants are unable to absorb adequate quantities of essential trace elements, and begin to languish, their foliage soon displaying the symptoms of iron deficiency by turning yellow. In acid soil, certain plants simply will not grow at all.

Obviously a rough idea of the alkalinity or acidity – the pH – of your compost is important. (The pH level is measured on a scale of 0 to 14: pH 7 is neutral, and readings above indicate alkalinity, whereas anything below is acid.) You can measure the pH of your compost using either a meter (expensive) or a disposable testing kit (cheap). Incidentally, for those with mathematical minds, pH is the negative

decimal logarithm of hydrogen ion concentration in moles per liter.

Neutral compost suits most plants. Adding lime will adjust acid composts, but, when they have become alkaline, there is not much you can do to reverse the process. Small quantities of soil which have become contaminated with lime or chalk can, to a limited extent, have their alkalinity reduced by sprinkling flowers of sulphur (the most widely available form of the element) onto the soil at a very approximate rate of $1/2$ cup per square yard. The process should be repeated every year in excessively limy soils.

The pH level fluctuates according to rainfall as well as to what treatment the soil has had. However, the changes are usually quite small, and the underlying status stays pretty well the same unless large volumes of lime have been added. In critical planting conditions it will be worth using a testing kit at the beginning of every growing season.

WATERING AND DRAINAGE

Adequate watering and good drainage are important for all aspects of gardening, but in containers they are crucial. Without it, root systems fail to develop, and plants look sick. Water must be able to run through compost in the planter, and then escape through a hole or holes in the bottom. Soil with a high clay content which is inclined to settle into an impermeable mass, so that the water cannot pass through, is unlikely to allow satisfactory drainage and should not be used.

Besides holes to let the water out, a container should have a layer of material along its floor which will aid drainage. In small pots, a handful or two of clay crocks or some coarse gravel will suffice. In larger planters, brick rubble or broken tiles may be better; place shingle on top of either to prevent compost from trickling into the spaces between the pieces.

After a number of years, the action of earthworms and sometimes of ants can clog drainage holes with powdered soil brought in from outside the container. Occasionally, a plant will send a taproot through the drainage holes and block them. When watering, therefore, always check that the containers' drains are running efficiently.

Drainage problems are easy to spot. If water stays on the surface of the compost for more than a few minutes after watering, if foliage begins to yellow and the compost feels clammy to the fingers, or if rotting odors develop, look to your drainage!

Watering is the most difficult job in the garden. The trouble is most of us have the wrong image of what it is. Imagine an old Hollywood musical. The star, if she is gardening, will invariably carry a tiny watering can with a large rose and sprinkle a few drops ineffectually onto the foliage of the plants, while she sings a sentimental ballad about her ideal man. Useless! But be careful: overwatering is almost as damaging as underwatering.

The way to avoid watering problems is to check the compost in the containers rather than merely look at the plants. Wilting plants *may* want water, but they could simply be responding to wind or high temperature, or even be suffering from waterlogging. Plunging your fingers down into the compost to feel its temperature and texture will tell you a lot about its condition. If it is dry or crumbly more than 1 inch down, it certainly needs watering.

HAND WATERING

Water must be poured onto the compost until it begins to run out of the drainage holes at the bottom. Failure to do this every time will result in a band of soluble salts being deposited part way down the container where the water stops each time you apply it. Eventually, this band becomes so concentrated it can rot roots.

In wet weather, unless there are days of continuous heavy rain, the chances are your containers will still need watering. If your neighbors are deputized to water in your absence, a little training session before you go should help to prevent spoiling a fine relationship.

BELOW Watering must be thorough. Each time, keep watering until the surplus runs out of the drainage holes. A sprinkling action can eventually cause roots to rot when a band of deposited soluble salts forms inside the pot.

CORRECT WATERING

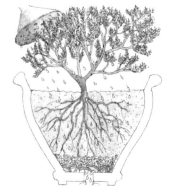

INCORRECT WATERING

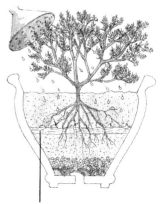

SOLUBLE SALTS

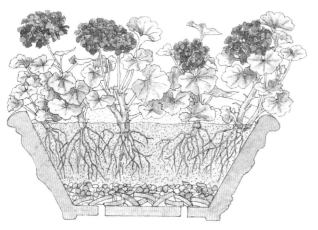

LEFT Holes in the bottom and a layer of broken crocks or bricks topped with coarse gravel or shingle are the easiest ways to insure good drainage for small and large containers respectively. The broken material prevents the drainage holes becoming blocked with compost.

Remember too, that containers which have been overfilled with compost may be difficult to water by hand. If the level of the compost is about 1 inch below the inside rim of the container, it is easier to introduce adequate quantities of water without it running straight off the top.

AUTOMATIC WATERING SYSTEMS

If you have a large number of containers, it may be advisable to automate. There are several systems available, each with its own advantages.

Overhead sprinkler lines Operated either by a small pump or mains pressure, this simple system is cheap to install. But it can cause leaf and flower damage, particularly when sprinkling in strong, direct sunlight. It is also wasteful of water,

and, in hard-water areas, can cause unsightly white staining on the foliage.

Trickle tubes From a main pipe a number of small tubes can feed water to each container, and will drip or trickle for as long as is necessary. One product consists of flexible hose which is porous enough to exude a slow ooze of water but also lets water be transported along its length. Laid in clustered containers, along window boxes or balcony troughs, below the surface of the compost, it delivers moisture directly to the root zone.

Capillary systems Large-scale nurseries make use of the capillary action of compost by setting their stock out on special aggregate which is supplied with water. The water finds its way up into the compost in the containers from the

bottom. This system can be adapted for domestic situations, provided the ground on which the containers stand is level. There are also capillary mats and trays which enable water to be supplied from the bottom without waterlogging the containers.

Feeding is possible through most automatic systems, and sophisticated set-ups will have automatic metering

ABOVE *Trickle tubes water grouped containers.*

devices to insure that the right nutrients get to the plants in the right quantities. However, when these go wrong, they usually go wrong in a big way, and can ruin the plants. There is no real substitute for keen observation and diligent husbandry.

ABOVE Containers on capillary matting supplied with water from a main pipe absorb the right amount of moisture, with or without added nutrients, to insure good growing conditions with minimal attention.

ABOVE Trickle tubes can be arranged to run from a main pipe to a number of different containers. Flow is adjusted to allow a steady drip of water which will keep compost moist without saturation.

PLANTING

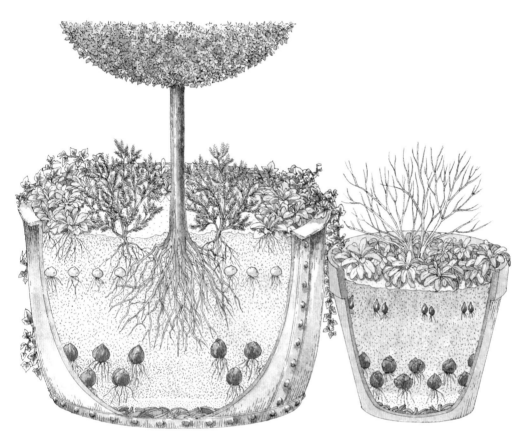

LEFT Bulbs should be planted in layers to insure a generous show. Tulips and daffodils can be planted to depths of 12 inches, but crocuses and bulbous irises prefer shallower planting.

Garden writers love to create a huge mystique over planting. Basically, all you do is dig a hole, and put the plant into it.

All plants dislike root disturbance, so it pays to plant with as little damage to the roots as possible. If these have become pot-bound, it may help to tease out some of them, particularly those which have wound around the bottom of the pot several times. But do be gentle and, if in doubt, leave the rootball alone: it will adjust itself naturally in time.

When the plant is in position, replace compost around it, and firm it in with both hands. Make sure that the compost is in contact with the root system, but take care not to crush or bruise the stems with your hand.

The hole you dig must be wide enough to accommodate all the roots without cramming and deep enough to hold the whole of the rootball (or pot-shaped root structure that you have just turned out of the pot). There are exceptions to these rules. Clematis and honeysuckles should be planted more deeply than they were when you bought them. Plant them deeply enough to bury the bottom two or three buds on the stem. These will eventually develop into extra leads and make a sturdier plant. It may be stating the obvious, but it is essential always to remove the original pot before planting the plant!

BULBS

It is almost impossible to plant bulbs too deep. Even if they are 12 inches below the soil surface, tulips will still emerge to flower well. Therefore, if bulbs are to be a permanent part of the scheme, plant them so deeply that they will not get in the way of subsequent summer planting. For density of flower, bulbs can be planted at several levels in the container. Even if they are on top of one another, the plants will emerge and flower well.

SEEDS

Sometimes annual seeds scattered on the tops of containers which have been previously planted with more substantial plants result in a pretty effect. Virginian stock (*Malcolmia maritima*) or *Iberis* are useful for this, but after germination be sure to remove any seedlings which are likely to spoil the more permanent plants.

CROWDED CONTAINERS

Planting into crowded containers is perfectly acceptable, provided care is taken not to spoil the roots of plants already there. A little tactful cutting back of the established plants' foliage will help to give the new introduction a head start, and will also help to compensate for root damage inflicted on them. There is a good rule to observe when planting: if a root is removed accidentally, a corresponding amount of top growth should also be removed. Thus, if you are transplanting mature plants and you estimate that about a third of the root has been lost, cut back a third of the top growth as well to ease the plant's task of re-establishing itself.

ABOVE *The opium poppies (Papaver somniferum) in the foreground are one example of the many annuals which can be sown in containers for speedy results in the summer. When they fade, they can be removed to make room for other plants.*

RIGHT *After their fine spring display, these narcissus hybrids can be replaced with a summer planting – perhaps geraniums, fuchsias, petunias or all three – and then replanted with bulbs or spring bedding the following fall to maintain the cycle.*

FEEDING

Green plants acquire most of their food through their leaves, by using sunlight to make carbohydrates from carbon dioxide, which they collect from the atmosphere, and from water, which they absorb from the soil through their roots. But to sustain these complicated life processes, they also need a number of chemical elements. These include nitrogen, phosphorus and potassium in relatively large amounts and other minerals – iron, calcium, manganese and magnesium among them – in much smaller quantities.

In the wild, these elements are abundant enough, but where plants are grown in artificial, contained conditions, such nutrients need to be added to the soil – a process called "feeding." With container gardening, feeding makes all the difference between triumph and disaster.

SOURCES OF NUTRIENTS

Natural nutrients Natural sources of nitrogen include such substances as animal manure or rock nitrates, and bone meal is very rich in phosphorus. But fish meal, hoof and horn meal, or the gruesome mix of blood, fish and bone meal provide all three major minerals. Though supposedly sterile, they are not at all pleasant to handle, and care with hygiene is essential.

For liquid feeding, some organic gardeners make up fetid solutions of dung, but purchased branded products derived from cattle manure or processed seaweed are easier to use.

Manufactured nutrients Ready-made compounds of all three major minerals are available and easy to use. Concentrations vary, but the manufacturer's packaging will usually state the recommended amounts to add to your compost.

One of the most labor-saving plantfood inventions has been the slow-release granule or tablet. The new compound fertilizer is manufactured in such a way that the nutrients are released slowly into the growing medium over a period of several months. This means that a single annual feed will take all but the hungriest plants right through the growing season.

FEED REGIMES

The general guidelines for feeding container plants are set out in the chart on the opposite page. Foliar feeding – spraying diluted liquid fertilizer directly onto the foliage – should be used with discretion. A quick tonic, it is a useful technique if plants are showing the signs of stress or hunger, such as yellow foliage or slower growth. The action, like that of champagne on an empty stomach, is instant but not sustained for very long. Manufactured liquid compounds or seaweed preparations make equally good foliar feeds, but to avoid leaf burn *never* spray in strong sunlight.

BELOW *Regular feeding insures plant health and constant color.*

	FEEDING CONTAINER-GROWN PLANTS	
PLANT	POINTS TO CONSIDER	ACTION
Trees and shrubs (permanent plants)	When planting, the aim is for rapid and sustained growth. Later, you may want the pace to be more sedate, but it is important not to underfeed to such an extent that the plants are malnourished and unhealthy.	At planting, incorporate fertilizer into the compost (or use a manufactured compost which already contains plantfood), and water in with a very weak solution of liquid fertilizer. The following season, or when the foliage shows signs of starvation, sprinkle slow-release granules onto the soil. Alternatively, use a slow-release fertilizer tab once a year in spring. Roses, which produce new wood and flower continuously, will need more frequent feeding and respond to regular foliar feeds.
Perennials (semipermanent plants)	These are shallow-rooted and fast-growing.	A few high-nitrogen feeds in the spring will insure vigorous growth, but, as soon as the plants approach maturity, switch to a potassium-rich feed to promote lusty flowering. Repeat every 14 to 21 days.
Alpines (permanent plants)	In troughs or sinks, alpines grow slowly, and need very little feeding.	A light annual dressing is favored by some growers, but I hardly ever feed mine.
Annuals and bedding (temporary plants)	These are the hungry ones. They must grow a full root system and large plant quickly, and perform in top gear for the whole season.	A generous feed at planting must be followed by regular feeding throughout the growing period. Liquid feeding every week is the simplest method.
Food crops	Generous feeding is essential. Members of the pea family have nitrogen-fixing bacteria on their roots, but they still need extra phosphorus and potassium.	Warm-weather plants such as tomatoes, sweet bell peppers, or eggplants, and fruit like strawberries need enough nitrogen to grow a large plant followed up with a high potassium fertilizer when they are mature to insure plenty of fruit. High-potassium tomato fertilizers, usually liquid, are as good for all fruiting vegetables – and flowers for that matter – as they are for tomatoes.

TRAINING AND PRUNING

Many climbing plants grow well in containers, but the methods of training and tying them need careful consideration because climbers tend to become top heavy. Trellis or pergola posts must be firmly anchored to the ground or to adjacent walls even if the planters are mobile.

There are dozens of different techniques for anchoring plants to walls, but the one I favor is the simple method of using vine eyes (nails with holes at their ends) or screw hooks with wire threaded through them. These are spaced about 18 inches apart and set so that wires can run *horizontally* along the wall. Thinner wires or pieces of string are then used to attach plants to the wire.

Some climbers are self-clinging and need no extra support – ivies, *Hydrangea anomala* subsp. *petiolaris*, or *Parthenocissis henryana* are examples. And some non-climbers – such as *Garrya elliptica*, *Fremontodendron californicum* and the Japanese quince

Chaenomeles x *speciosa* – make superb wall plants which are lovely in themselves and through which true climbers can be encouraged to grow.

Climbers in containers need more severe pruning than their counterparts in open ground because their root systems are more limited, and cannot therefore support a large mass of top growth without looking starved. Several genera, especially clematis and honeysuckles, are happy in full light as long as their roots are cool, so their containers should be sited in as shady a spot as possible, even if their occupants climb into the sun.

SMALL TREES AND LARGE SHRUBS

Containerized trees and large shrubs are seldom able to grow to their full potential, and must be kept to a reasonable size, but tactless pruning looks horrible. The sign of an indifferent pruner is the "neat bobble" syndrome, in which bushes are robbed of their natural shape and shorn into roundheaded knobs.

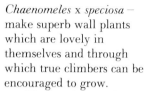

LEFT *By using a spherical framework of wire, the ivy in the foreground has been trained into a near-perfect globe.*

RIGHT *Topiary has turned shrubs into living sculptures which create a structure in harmony with the furniture.*

Pruning is not easy, but the aim should be to retain as much of the characteristic shape of the plant as possible. Spring-flowering shrubs can have their flowering branches removed as soon as they have faded so that new leads spring from the base, although this is not so easy with rhododendrons or azaleas. With other shrubs you will need all your aesthetic skills. Treat the plant like a living sculpture: remove a branch at a time, step back to see what you have done, size up the plant and decide which bit to cut off next. Above all, know when to stop.

TOPIARY

Having scorned the "neat bobble," it may seem contradictory to point out that plants trimmed into shapes or hedges make fine container subjects. Bay trees, box plants or hollies clipped into formal patterns are quite different from shrubs which have been hacked into submission. There is much skill in their maintenance, usually involving one or more clips per year to keep them in shape. Purchasing such plants, ready-shaped, is costly, but to grow them yourself from scratch takes many years. All plants which are heavily pruned need feeding to compensate for the material removed.

RIGHT *Climbers like the passion flower can easily become top-heavy.*

Shaping a mophead
Stake the shrub's main stem upright in several places.

Cut off lower side shoots flush with the main stem as the shrub grows.

Pinch out the terminal bud to stop growth and let a ball of foliage develop.

Trim the branches of the lower half of the ball to form an umbrella.

Training a spiral
Wind young conifers round a stake securing them in position at intevals.

For ivy, attach a stiff wire spiral to the top and bottom of a stake, then trail the plant around it.

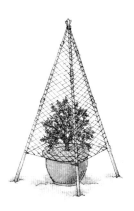

Creating a pyramid
Place a pyramid-shaped frame of wire mesh over the young shrub.

As the shrub grows, trim protruding sprigs just past the mesh so as to conceal the wire frame.

When a full pyramid shape is achieved, remove the frame and trim regularly to preserve the outline.

For a ball, let the main stem grow up, then pinch it out. Trim the side shoots that develop into a sphere.

PROPAGATION

Some gardeners get their kicks from propagating (plants, I mean, not their own kind, though that can be fun too!), and find tinkering about with seed and cuttings a source of deep satisfaction. Others dislike the production side of horticulture and buy all their plants in. Propagating your own can be beneficial.
● It is cheaper than buying new plants.
● There is often a wider choice of seed than of commercially grown plants.
● It enables you to swap rooted cuttings or seed with fellow gardeners.
● Cherished species can be multiplied at home.

EQUIPMENT

The ultimate is a mist propagation system, which provides a controlled humid environment automatically, combined with hot benches in a generously proportioned greenhouse. The next best is a small greenhouse, preferably featuring soil-warming equipment. Moving down the scale, a simple cold frame will allow some propagation.

If you lack all those facilities, you can still raise plants with a windowsill propagator or even just a windowsill. If you have no garden and limited space, or if massed pots with infant plants on every windowsill falls short of your idea of good interior decor, there are fluorescent tubes designed to sustain plant growth which can transform a lumber room or basement into a growing zone.

TECHNIQUES

Assuming that you have at least minimal facilities, propagation falls into the following categories.

Division A very easy method, it can be used on any plant with a running rootstock, or with a number of rosettes which will divide. Lift the plants and tease them apart into small pieces – each consisting of at least one good shoot and a set of roots – and re-plant immediately. Be sure to clean up the divisions by trimming off any weak, old or dying material.

Layering Good for shrubs and climbers, this method is just as easy as division, but can take ages. A piece of stem near ground level is anchored down so that part of the bark is buried. Roots will develop at that point, and a new plant is thus formed. Scratching or wounding the bark first will hasten the process.

Shrubs or trees with erect stems can be air-layered. A bunch of damp moss is fixed at a point where the bark has been wounded and is held in place until roots have formed. Box-like devices are available to contain the moss and close over the branch. The moss must be kept moist at all times.

Stem cuttings These can be taken from soft growth (of perennials or shrubs) in midsummer or from semi-ripe shoots (of woody plants) in the fall.

With bottom heat in a propagator, soft-growth cuttings should root within a few weeks, and provide young, healthy plants by the fall. There are hormone preparations to hasten root development. It is important to keep the air around the cuttings as humid as possible. Outdoors, a translucent cover will help, but inside, if you have no windowsill propagator, a polyetheline bag, inflated and tied to enclose the pot, should be enough.

Semi-ripe cuttings are selected in the fall from young shoots which have become woody in the last few weeks. They can be inserted directly into the ground or into a container filled with gritty compost, and left in a cool spot until growth has begun the following spring.

LEFT Seeds and cuttings need gentle warmth, a humid atmosphere and protection from sudden changes in temperature to thrive. A simple windowsill propagator will provide these conditions at very little cost – the electricity consumed daily is minimal. A seed tray enclosed in a polyetheline bag is almost as effective and even cheaper.

The resulting young plants will need different quarters in full light and more airy surroundings when they have germinated or rooted in the propagator, so a greenhouse or coldframe is also useful.

Division

Tease rootstocks apart by hand and subdivide into small sections. Make sure each piece has viable roots and at least one healthy shoot. If they are congested, use a fork to separate them or cut them through with a knife.

Layering

Scrape some of the bark off the lower section of a branch or shoot before anchoring it in the soil. Stiff branches may need to be secured with wire or a rock. When roots have developed, cut the branch from the parent plant and replant it.

Air-layering

Select a healthy shoot. Make a diagonal cut half through the stem, wedge the wound open with moist sphagnum moss, then wrap moss or compost around the seam, and secure it with polyetheline. When roots form, remove and plant the shoot.

Stem cutting

Cut a healthy, non-flowering shoot through a node (where the leaf joins the stem), and remove lower leaves so that none will touch the soil. Insert the cutting into gritty compost, and place in a propagator or coldframe until rooted.

Root cutting

Lift mature plants in winter and remove sections of root. Cut these into short pieces, arranging them either vertically or sideways and covering them with compost. Make sure the upper portion is just below the surface.

Root cuttings This method is useful for perennials with fleshy roots. In winter, shake soil off the roots of the plants, snip the thickest roots into short lengths, and insert them into a seed tray or pot filled with gritty compost. The root sections can be vertical or horizontal, but must be covered with compost and kept moist but not too wet.

Seed There are so many methods that it simply is not possible, here, to do much more than outline good practice and warn of pitfalls.

Germination problems usually stem from stale seed or incorrect sowing temperature. Some plants must have frost to split their seed coats and permit the absorption of water. Others need heat. Therefore, read the instructions on the package or, if these are not helpful, find out what the plant's natural habitat is like. A Mexican salvia is unlikely to need frost to sprout, but a Himalayan primula certainly will.

Hygiene, or lack of it, is the most common cause of disease, particularly the condition known as "damping off." If seedlings start to die for no obvious reason, remove the offending batch and, if the remainder are big enough to handle, prick them out and move them elsewhere.

Aftercare is important, particularly where seed-raising is an improvised affair using windowsills. There is seldom enough

ABOVE Kalanchoe blossfeldiana *reflect the reddish color of their background. They can be multiplied by rooting stem cuttings in spring.*

light for optimum growth, and yet a window may have too much direct sun at certain times of the day. In these circumstances, the sooner young seedlings can be placed in pots and put outside, the better they will perform.

OVERWINTERING

Winter brings with it two dilemmas: what to grow for winter interest, and what to do with plants which need protection during winter. The first question has been answered in the preceding chapters. There are several ways of overcoming the second. Wrapping up all the containers in burlap and straw or throwing all the plants away are two extreme solutions, but how awful the garden will look, and what a waste! Annuals will die, of course, to be replaced with bulbs and spring bedding, but tender perennials can be preserved during the winter in two ways.

Cuttings Take cuttings in late summer and keep them indoors during winter as small house-plants, setting them outside again as soon as the risk of frost has passed the following year.

Rootstock Lift the mature plants, allow them to die back and preserve the roots in a dormant state until the following spring. To keep them alive but not growing, you will need a cold but frost-free store. Dahlias are usually stored this way, but almost anything with a robust, tuberous rootstock will respond to similar treatment. *Salvia patens* or *Cosmos atrosanguineus*, for example, are easy to keep during winter like this; so are chrysanthemums. Check the roots occasionally for rot and water sparingly if they are too dry. In spring, the whole root can be replanted and placed outdoors, but

more vigorous offspring can be obtained by starting the tubers into growth, then removing the strong basal shoots which emerge and striking these as cuttings.

Tender summer bulbs, in particular gladiolus, *Tigridia* or acidantheras, always need to be stored frost-free, but tulips and daffodils are happier left alone in their containers to take whatever the weather throws at them. Large bulbs like agapanthus or crinums can be lifted for storage, but will flower better if there is some means of bringing the container indoors intact.

Tender shrubs are also best brought under cover, perhaps into a greenhouse specially designed for the purpose. Depending on what species are grown, the cost of heating should not be enormous. All the Mediterranean plants, for example, will survive quite happily as long as they are kept just above freezing point so there is no need to insure a higher minimum than 32°F.

Taking containers out again in spring always requires a certain amount of circumspection. Night frost can be damaging to young shoots and, where early growth has been rapid under glass, plant tissue will be soft and easily bruised by wind. Since it could take several weeks for the plants to recover and adapt to the conditions outdoors, if in doubt, it is important to leave them under glass for a little longer.

ABOVE *Although a number of evergreens and winter plants can be grown to maintain structural and incidental interest in the garden, there is bound to be a surplus of containers which must be set aside until spring.*

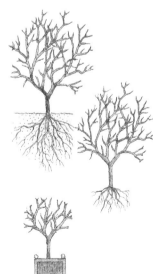

RIGHT When shrubs or trees are lifted from a large container to be stored indoors through winter, some root damage is inevitable. To compensate, trim off about one third of the top growth, taking care to retain the essential shape.

PESTS, DISEASES AND DISORDERS

CENTIPEDE

LADYBUG AND NYMPH

ADULT LACEWING

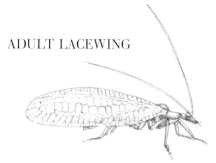

ADULT
SYRPHUS FLY

LEFT *Centipedes hunt for small slugs and insect pests at night. Ladybugs and their nymphs live on aphids, consuming huge numbers in a lifetime. The larvae of both syrphus flies and lacewings are also voracious consumers of most kinds of aphid pests.*

In light of the current trend for more ecologically sound gardening, a very welcome change after decades of heavy chemical dependence, we need to take a fresh and rather more holistic look at plant diseases and disorders.

Sooner or later, every garden suffers from pests or diseases. Some of these are incurable and others so debilitating or disfiguring that the impulse to pull up and discard the affected plants is almost irresistible. But the great majority are minor and can be tolerated, or are easy to eradicate with or without chemical aids. The decision that each individual gardener has to make is whether or not to use any chemicals and, if they are to be used, how often and extensively. Below are two different approaches to disease control.

For what it is worth, my own philosophy is to use chemicals as infrequently as possible but to resort to them when other means of control are impossible. I spray my roses with a prophylactic fungicide because I would be unable to control mildew, black spot and rust without doing so, but I refrain from any other form of chemical preventive treatment.

GREEN METHOD

The key is good husbandry. Healthy plants which are growing strongly are less likely to succumb to pests or diseases than are poor, weak specimens. Careful, close observation of the plants will pay dividends, especially if you can anticipate problems. There are plenty of insects which are large enough to be picked or washed off without

any sort of pesticide. Caterpillars, sawfly grubs, some aphids and pollen beetles come into this category. Try to discover the cause of fungal disease – more often a management fault than anything else – and attack that rather than the disease.

Choose the right plants for the right site. Always select varieties which are known for their disease-resistance. Rose mildew, for example, is far more likely on a warm wall, so select a mildew-resistant variety or grow something different on that site.

Some plants have their own, in-built pesticide activity. *Tagetes patula*, for instance, is said to produce a root exudate which can be absorbed by other plants and will then act as a natural systemic pesticide against

cabbage whitefly. Thus, tomatoes and tagetes growing together in the same container can look pretty and keep themselves free of the pest.

There are ecologically acceptable pesticides, and these include biological control (with parasites) and certain naturally produced products, although why the naturally derived poison derris is acceptable to ecologists and the synthetic pyrethrins (which are chemically similar to the poison produced by the pyrethrum plant) are not mystifies me. The chart opposite illustrates the use of "green" pest control.

NOT-QUITE-SO-GREEN METHOD

Adopt all the techniques described in the green method but, without being an irresponsible earth-wrecker and only when really necessary, also use chemicals which, in moderation, can make the garden healthier. A monthly spray with a systemic fungicide makes a huge difference to the appearance and health of roses; painting individual perennial weeds

with glyphosate eliminates them without disturbing any of the other plants nearby; judicious use of slug bait can save young annuals. How much damage does that do to the environment? The sensible approach, then, is to resort to chemical aids only when absolutely necessary but to try every other possible method first. As with all horticultural matters, good husbandry, with attention to detail, is the key to success.

ABOVE *Pest control is essential to insure satisfactory yields, especially when food crops are being grown. Organic methods include growing French marigolds (tagetes) with tomatoes. The insect-repelling chemicals exuded by the marigolds' roots are absorbed by the tomato plants with a resulting drop in numbers of insect pests. The pretty flowers are a colorful bonus for the vegetable patch.*

PEST CONTROL FOR ORGANIC GARDENING

PREVENTION

Purchasing plants
Always scrutinize plants before purchase, and refuse to buy any which have evidence of pest or disease damage. Look for signs of thrips – discolored areas on petals or misshapen flowers – and for leaf damage, discoloration or yellowing caused by a virus.

Growing conditions
Insure healthy plants by providing the best possible growing conditions for them.

Hygiene Discard any diseased plant material by burning, if possible. Be scrupulous with your plant hygiene by cleaning out pots before reusing them, removing all dead leaf litter, using clean compost.

Viruses Be especially vigilant in your watch for aphids. These are the virus carriers and when a plant has a virus, it cannot be cured.

Natural control
Encourage natural predators. Many insects devour aphids. Centipedes kill other harmful insects.

CURE

Mechanical control
Wash off or sponge off insect pests as soon as you notice them.

Pesticides Use natural-based pesticides such as derris dust. Other "safe" pesticides include soft or green soap, quassia, which kills aphids but not ladybirds, and pyrethrum.

Fungicides Sulfur and commercial compounds containing copper are widely used by organic gardeners for controlling fungi; Bordeaux Mixture, a compound of copper sulfate and calcium hydroxide, is popular.

Biological control
The parasitic wasp encarsia lives on whitefly, and can be used to control this pest. Red spider mite can be kept in check by the parasitic mite *Phytoseiulis persimllis.* Bacteria such as *Bacillus thuringiensis* can be used to kill certain caterpillars by spraying them onto the affected crop. These biological controls are available at garden centers.

DIRECTORY
OF USEFUL
PLANTS

Since the number of species and varieties suitable for container culture runs into tens of thousands, there is only room here to mention a small sample. What follows is a selection of plants with proven track records as reliable subjects for growing in containers. Some are fully frost-hardy, others are more suitable for warm climates.

A list of essential details is supplied for each entry in every section but, since for most entries plant genera – rather than individual species – are given, some of the dimensions and cultural preferences are generalized, and therefore should be regarded only as guidelines. Where genera vary a great deal and therefore require a wide range of growing conditions, some symbols have been omitted as they would be unhelpful.

Before finalizing any plant selection, check the specific species and/or variety details against your planting requirements. A complete explanation of the symbols at the top of each entry appears on the following page. The key which appears at the bottom of each page is necessarily a shorthand version, and serves simply as a reminder of the symbols' meanings. Readers are recommended to check their selections against the key on the following page.

LEFT *Decorative foliage, a trailing habit and bright, long-lasting flowers render the common nasturtium, a popular container subject.*

KEY

HARDINESS

❄ = fully hardy in frost down to 10°F
(Zone 8)

☚ = slightly tender and not happy below
30°F (Zone 10)

⌂ = not frost-hardy and not happy below
41°F

HABIT

◗ = growing erect

◐ = trailing, climbing or mat-forming

❦ = rounded or bushy

The word "various" is used to indicate a range of habit.

DIMENSIONS

Intended only as a very rough guide, I have listed optimum sizes when growing in the ground rather than maximum proportions. The ultimate size of most plants, especially of trees and shrubs, depends very much on the size of the container. The word "various" indicates a range of dimensions.

ABOVE *Handsome evergreen foliage and a long flowering season make abutilon a valuable genus for container gardening. Other varieties have variegated foliage and a wide range of flower colors.*

ASPECT

☼ = full sun

◗ = partial shade

● = full shade

The preferred aspect comes first, followed by viable alternative(s). Thus ☼ ◗ means prefers sun but tolerates partial shade.

SOIL CONDITIONS

D = dry

M = moist

<pH7 = needs acid soil

Preferred soil condition comes first, followed by viable alternative.

PROPAGATION METHOD

Sd = seed

Ct = cuttings

Dv = division

The most usual methods are given in order of preference.

BEST SEASON

Sp = spring

Su = summer

Fa = fall

Wi = winter

Ay = all year

Indicates the season during which the plants look their best.

TREES AND SHRUBS

ABUTILON

ɫ ◊ 🜂 various ☼ D SdCt SuFa

Flowers, foliage. Evergreen. Mallow relatives, many with well-marked foliage and brightly colored flowers, each with a prominent central column of stamens. *A. pictum* has cream stippling on foliage and orange, veined flowers. *A. vitifolium* grows much larger – to 12 feet on a wall – and has blue to mauve flowers. Forms of *A. hybridum* have crimson or yellow flowers.

ACER

✳ ɫ various ◗ ● ☼ M Sd Ay

Maple. Foliage. Valuable genus of trees and shrubs which provide shape and outline as well as foliage color. Small maples include *A. palmatum* and *A. japonicum*, both of which have many fine cultivars. *A. griseum*, a shade lover, has papery bark. Some species are susceptible to spring frosts and cold winds. Tougher species include *A. pseudoplatanus* "Brilliantissimum," with shrimp-pink buds in spring, and *A. negundo*, the box elder, which has variegated forms.

BETULA

✳ ◊ 20 feet +☼ ◗ ● M SdCt Ay

Birch. Foliage, stems. Useful trees which can be kept small in containers. The young stems and outlines of *Betula utilis* and *B. u.* subsp. *jacquemontii* are especially graceful, and become gray, sandy pink or silvery white as they mature.

CALLUNA

✳ ◊ 🜂 18 inches ☼ M <pH7 CtSd Ay

Scotch heather. Flowers, foliage. Pink, rose purple, white. Robust and reliable, providing flowers from midsummer to late fall, many varieties also having attractive foliage. Examples: "Alba Plena" and "Loch Turret" (white); "Beechwood Crimson" and "Darkness" (purple red); "Elsie Purnell" (pink). Colored

ABOVE Acer palmatum *"Rubrum,"* a dwarf maple, makes a shapely container tree.

foliage varieties include "Beoley Gold" (gold foliage, white flowers); "Fred J. Chapple" (coral foliage, pink flowers); "Multicolor" (yellow, orange and green foliage, pink flowers).

CAMELLIA

✳ ɫ ♀ various ● ◗ M <pH7 Ct Sp Ay

Tea tree. Flowers, foliage. Pink, red, white. Important for the lustrous beauty of their leaves as well as their blooms. Hardiness varies, so choose the right varieties for your climate. Tender varieties, bred from *C. reticulata*, include "Butterfly Wings" (semi-double, rose pink) and "Robert Fortune" (double, deep red). Hardy forms include *C.* x *williamsii* hybrids, such as "Donation" (semi-double, pink) and "Bow Bells" (single, pink), and *C. japonica* hybrids like "Adolphe Audussen" (semi-double, dark red) and "Alba Simplex" (single, white).

CHAENOMELES
✳ ♀ 8 feet ○ ☽ DM Ct WiSp

Japanese quince. Flowers. Red, pink, white. Late winter blossom, followed by edible green-yellow fruits on shrubs which can be trained as screens or grow freestanding. Cultivars include "Nivalis" (white), "Crimson and Gold" (blood red with bright golden stamens) and "Pink Lady."

CHOISYA
⸖ ♀ 6 feet ○ D Ct SpSu

Mexican orange. Flowers, foliage, fragrance. White. Lustrous evergreen with three-lobed leaves and white, waxy, fragrant flowers in late spring and again in the fall.

CISTUS
✳ ♀ various ○ D SdCt SpSu

Rockrose. Flowers. Pink, white. Several species are useful in a hot, dry corner. *C. Ladanifer has* sticky, aromatic foliage and huge white flowers with dark central spots. *C.* x *corbariensis*, with smaller foliage, is pure white and *C.* x *purpureus* is rosy pink with darker markings.

CITRUS
⌂ ⸖ ⬙ Various ○ D cpH7 SdCt Ay

Orange, Lemon. Foliage, flowers, fruit. White. Evergreen shrubs with aromatic foliage, fragrant in flower and bearing brilliantly colored fruit. All worth growing but lemons and the dwarf Chinese orange *Citrus mitis* (x *Citrofortunella mitis*), with its copious flowering and tiny fruits, are especially decorative.

CONVOLVULUS CNEORUM
⸖ ⬙ 2 feet ○ D CtSd SpSuFa

Foliage, flowers. The plant with the best silver color – its foliage being almost metallic in certain lights. The growth is bushy, the flowers pale pink in the bud, opening to white with pale yellow centers.

ABOVE Choisya, *the Mexican orange, is a fragrantly evergreen aromatic shrub.*

DORYCNIUM HIRSUTUM
⸖ ⬙ 12 inches ○ D SdCt Ay

Foliage, flowers. Small shrub with silver, three-lobed foliage and downy flowers which are pink in the bud and open white. Seeds freely in hot, dry conditions.

ERICA
✳ ♀ ⬗ 12 inches ○ DM SdCt Ay

Heather. Flowers, foliage. Pink, white, mauve. Large genus with many varieties valuable for container use. *E. arborea is* white and grows large; *E. herbacea* (syn. *E. carnea*) comes in all three colors and flowers in winter. Most ericas prefer neutral or acid soil, but *E. terminalis* and *E. herbacea* will grow in lime.

EUCALYPTUS
⸖ ⬙ various ○ D Sd Ay

Gum. Foliage. Huge genus of Australasian natives with mainly blue-gray foliage and tufty flowers whose colors include cream, red and pink. Juvenile foliage differs from leaves on mature branches. *E. gunnii* and *E. niphophila* are among the hardiest and most decorative species.

✳ hardy | ⸖ slightly tender | ⌂ tender | ⬙ erect | ⬗ trailing | ♀ bushy | ○ sun | ☽ partial shade

ABOVE *Mop-head varieties of hydrangea make excellent, but thirsty, container subjects.*

FICUS
⌂ ⸸ various DM SdCt Ay

Fig. Foliage, fruit. Species with large, three- or five-lobed leaves provides edible fruit. Tropical species of garden merit include *F. benjamina*, which can be trained and clipped, and *F. elastica*, whose foliage is huge.

FUCHSIA
⸸ various ☼ ☽ M CtSd SuFa

Flowers. Pink, red, mauve, purple-blue. One of the most widely grown container plants with many different forms. Flowering begins in early summer and continues into late fall. *F. magellanica* is the hardiest, with small, narrow red flowers.

HYDRANGEA
⸸ ❊ various ☼ ☽ M Ct Ay

Flowers, foliage. Deciduous shrubs with long-lasting flowers. Species include *H. quercifolia* – cream flowers and fine fall leaf color – but the many cultivars of *H. macrophylla* are the most widely grown. These are white, pink or blue, and include "Blue Bonnet" and "Generale Vicomtesse de Vibray" (pink).

LAURUS NOBILIS
⸸ ⸱ 10 feet+ ● ☽ D Ct Ay

Bay. Foliage. Evergreen, aromatic shrubs which can be clipped into shapes. Small, starry, cream yellow flowers in spring. Not suitable for deep frost.

LAVANDULA
❊ ⸸ various ☼ D CtSd Su

Lavender. Flowers, foliage. Blue, lavender, white. *Lavandula angustifolia* has silvery foliage and fragrant flowers; "Vera," "Munstead" and "Hidcote" are good cultivars. *L. stoechas* and *L. lanata* thrive in hot, dry conditions but are less hardy.

LAVATERA
❊ ⸸ ♀ various ☼ D SdCt Su

Tree mallow. Flowers. Rapid, free-flowering shrubs with large flowers produced for most of the summer. *L. olbia* "Rosea" is pink and *L. thuringiaca* "Barnsley" is white, turning silvery pink, with red centers.

PRUNUS
❊ various SpFa Ay

Cherry, plum, laurel. Flower, fruit, foliage, bark. Pink, white. Huge genus of flowering trees and shrubs.
Small shrubs Dwarf, flowering species include *Prunus triloba*, *P. mume* and *P. tenella*. Evergreen laurels, useful for winter interest, include *P. laurocerasus* "Otto Luyken," a dwarf with many white flowers in spring. *P.* x *cistena* is a dwarf with purple foliage and pale pink flowers.
Larger trees Includes many ornamental cherries such as "Kursar" (pink, fall color) and "Amanogawa" with upright habit and mid-pink flowers. This group also includes almonds, apricots, peaches, plums and edible cherries, all of which will grow well in large containers. The morello cherry will produce fruit in shade.

● shade │ D dry │ M moist │ <pH7 needs acid soil │ Sd seed │ Ct cuttings │ Dv division

PUNICA GRANATUM
⌂ ♀ 8 feet ☼ D CtSd Ay

Pomegranate. Flowers, foliage. Scarlet-orange flowers with crushed petals produced for much of the summer, followed by heavy fruits. The dwarf *P. granatum* var. *nana* is a decorative variety.

RHODODENDRON
⊱ ✳ various M <pH7 ● ☽ SdCt Ay

Flowers, foliage. Mainly evergreen shrubs or trees with many colorful species from tiny bushes to large trees with huge leathery leaves. Many dwarf species adapt to container life, and most are shade-tolerant but need a peaty, acid compost. *R. yakushimanum* and its hybrids are among the easiest to grow, but there are others with flowers ranging from blue, through shades of pink and red, to salmon and primrose yellow, many being scented. Examples: "Azuma-kagami" (a pink azalea type); *R. calostrotum* (blue foliage, red flowers); *R. kiusianum* (mauve purple); "Pink Drift" (very dwarf).

BELOW *This modern hybrid bush rose performs well in a half barrel. The silver artemisia makes a charming companion.*

ROBINIA
✳ ⌁ 12 feet+ ☼ ☽ D Ct SpSuFa

Honey locust. Foliage, flowers, outline. Trees which tolerate confined roots and have late-emerging, pinnate foliage. *R. pseudoacacia* "Frisia" has golden leaves and *R. hispida* blossoms with rose-pink peaflowers.

ROSA
✳ various ☼ Ct SuFa

Rose. Flowers, fruit, foliage. A vast range of garden shrubs, many of which are excellent container plants. The more compact, slower growing varieties are best for smaller pots but sizeable shrub roses will thrive in roomy containers. Repeat-flowering hybrids are best, and among old roses *Rosa* "Old Blush China" and "Hermosa" are reliable. Of modern varieties, the dwarf, cluster-flowered bush type – known as "patio roses" – are ideal for container use. Examples: "Wee Jock" (red); "Rugul" (yellow); "Sweet Magic" (orange); "Drummer Boy" (crimson, scented). See also Climbers and Trailers section.

SALIX
✳ various ☼ ☽ CtSd Ay

Willow. Twigs, catkins, foliage. An easy genus, tolerant of shade and poor soil. Species with fine, silvery foliage include *S. lanata*, *S. helvetica* and *S. glauca*. Catkins are seldom better than on *S. hastata*, but *S. fargesii* has polished red twigs and bold summer foliage.

SANTOLINA
✳ ♀ 2½ feet ☼ D CtSd Ay

Cotton lavender. Flowers, foliage. Yellow. Drought-loving, low-growing bushes with silver or green foliage and yellow button flowers in summer. *S. pinnata* subsp. *neapolitana* has sulfur-yellow flowers and *S. rosmarinifolia* (syn. *S. virens*) deep green feathery foliage. The commonest species, with mustard flowers, is *S. chamaecyparissus*.

CLIMBERS AND TRAILERS

CLEMATIS
✻ ◑ various ☼ ◗ M CtSd SpSuFa

Traveler's joy, old man's beard. Huge genus of climbers which flower at various seasons and come in many colors but predominantly blue, mauve and pink. Cool, moist rootrun essential. Many are happy in containers.

Montana types Pink or white flowers in spring. Examples: *C. chrysocoma* (pale pink); *C. montana* "Tetrarose" (deep pink); *C. chrysocoma* var. *sericea* (white).

Alpina/macropetala types Nodding blue, pink or white flowers in spring with further blooms in late summer. Examples: *C. alpina* "Ruby;" *C. alpina* "Frances Rivis" (blue); *C. alpina* var. *sibirica* "White Moth."

C. viticella cultivars. White, blue or purple-red flowers in summer, plants need cutting back each year. Examples: "Alba Luxurians" (white); "Royal Velours" (purple-red); "Etoile Violette" (deep purple violet).

Large-flowered hybrids Blue, pink or white flowers in spring (early) or summer to fall (late). Early-flowering hybrids must not be pruned but the late varieties can be cut back hard each spring. Early examples: "Marie Boisselot" (white); "H.F. Young" (pale blue). Late examples: "Jackmanii" (royal blue); "Hagley Hybrid" (pink).

Orientalis types Mostly yellow flowers with good seedheads. Examples: "Bill Mackenzie;" *C. tangutica*; *C. orientalis.*

CONVOLVULUS
☽ ✻ various ☼ MD SdCt SuFa

Flowers. Blue, purple, pink, white. Herbaceous climbers with saucer flowers. *C. sabatius* (syn. *C. mauritanicus*) produces waves of bright, purple-blue flowers. *Ipomoea* is a similar genus: vigorous plants with large, "loudspeaker" flowers in blue, mauve or wine red.

RIGHT Convolvulus mauritanicus, *a tender summer perennial, produces an endless supply of violet-blue "loudspeaker" flowers.*

ECCREMOCARPUS SCABER
☽ ◑ 10 feet ☼ DM Sd SuFa

Flowers. Yellow, orange, red. Rapid herbaceous climber with clusters of tubular flowers in summer and fall.

GLECHOMA HEDERACEA "VARIEGATA"
✻ ◑ 6 inches ☼ ◗ M Ct Ay

Ground ivy. Foliage, flowers. Trailing stems which root where they touch the ground. Cream and green, nettle-like foliage with little blue flowers in spring. Good for hanging baskets.

HEDERA
✻ ◑ various ● ◗ MD Ct Ay

Ivy. Foliage, screening. Valuable for trailing, climbing on screens or walls or for training into shapes. Many colored leaf forms of *Hedera helix*, including "Goldheart" (bold yellow variegations); "Heise" (gray-green foliage, white variegations); "Buttercup" (leaves turn yellow in sun). *H. canariensis* is slightly tender, but the variety "Gloire de Marengo" has gray and white foliage. *H. colchica* has enormous leaves, and "Sulphur Heat" is variegated.

● shade | D dry | M moist | <pH7 needs acid soil | Sd seed | Ct cuttings | Dv division

JASMINUM
✳ ⚑ ⚑ various to 12 feet ○ ◗ D Ct Ay

Jasmine. Flowers, foliage, fragrance, screening. Vigorous climbers with green stems and often fragrant flowers produced over a long period. Winter jasmine, *J. nudiflorum*, is fully hardy with yellow flowers in winter. The summer-flowering *J. polyanthum* and *J. officinale* are both white-flowered, highly scented but less hardy.

LAPAGERIA ROSEA
✳ ⚑ 10 feet ● M <pH7 CtSd Su

Chilean bellflower. Flowers, foliage. Evergreen foliage and tubular, waxy red flowers in late summer and fall.

LATHYRUS
✳ ⚑ various ○ M Sd Su

Sweet pea. Flowers, fragrance, screening. Purple, mauve, white, pink, red, orange. The annual sweet pea, *Lathyrus odoratus*, besides being a fine container plant, has several perennial relatives, of which *L. sylvestris* – purple and mauve – is one of the easiest to grow.

LONICERA
✳ various ● ◗ M CtSd SpSuWi

Honeysuckle. Flowers, foliage, fragrance, screening. Cream, yellow, orange, red, white. Large genus of valuable climbers which prefer shade but, if their roots are cool, will perform well in containers. Species include *L. periclymenum* and its cultivars, flowering from midspring to late summer, and the summer-flowering *L. japonica* "Aureo-reticulata," with its gold netted leaf, and the brilliantly colored *L.* "Dropmore Scarlet."

PASSIFLORA
✳ ⚑ 20 feet + ○ D SdCt Ay

Passion flower. Flowers, foliage, screening. Red, purple, mauve. Vigorous but frost-tender climbers with extraordinary flowers and edible fruits. *P. caerulea is* the hardiest, with mauve, white and green flowers all summer. *P. coccinea* is glowing red, *P.* x *exoniensis* is rose pink.

RHODOCHITON ATROSANGUINEUM
⌂ ❦ 10 feet ○ M SdCt Su

Flowers. Pink and purple-black. Vigorous herbaceous climber with masses of elegant, hanging flowers Their calyces are wine pink but the tubular, four-lipped petals are deep purple to black. Not suitable for cold gardens.

LEFT *Vigorous, frost-tender passion flowers need to be kept in check in confined areas.*

ROSA
✳ various ☼ Ct SuFa

Rose. Flowers, screening. Ramblers are too rampaging for containers but climbers such as "Lady Hillingdon" (apricot), "Guinée" (maroon), "Golden Showers" and "Climbing Cécile Brunner" (pink) enjoy container life. "Nozomi" and "The Fairy" – both pale pink to white – are good for trailing over pots.

TROPAEOLUM
✳ ⊱ ◐ ☼ ◗ DM Sd Su

Nasturtium. Flowers, foliage. Red, orange, yellow. Apart from the easy and invasive common nasturtium, *T. majus,* there are more restrained container species, including *T. peregrinum* (yellow) and *T. speciosum* (scarlet).

VINCA
✳ ⊱ ◐ various ◗ ● MD DvCt Ay

Periwinkle. Foliage, flowers. Blue, wine-red, white. Trailers rather than climbers, with glossy evergreen foliage and symmetrical flowers. *V. minor* has the best range of flower color but *V. major* is a more rambunctious trailer. Both have variegated leaf forms.

VITIS
✳ ⊱ ◐ 10 feet + ☼ D CtDv Ay

Vine. Foliage, fruit, screening. The hardy grape-vine, *V. vinifera,* is highly decorative with large, soft green leaves; there is a purple leaf form, *V. v.* "Purpurea." Other species include *V. coignetiae* (crimson glory vine), whose huge, russet-backed leaves turn red and orange in the fall.

RIGHT Vinca major *is one of several species of periwinkle, which are valuable for their glossy, evergreen trailing foliage and abundance of spring and early-summer flowers. There are garden forms with white, purple, and light or dark blue flowers, as well as several species sporting variegated foliage.*

WISTERIA
✳ ♀ 20 feet + ☼ D Sd SpSu

Flowers, foliage, screening. Violet-blue, white. Long-lived climbers with lovely racemes of mostly lavender-blue flowers in spring and fresh foliage all summer. *W. sinensis* flowers freely but *W. floribunda* has longer racemes. Cultivars include "Black Dragon," a dark blue, semi-double.

ZEBRINA (TRADESCANTIA)
◻ ◐ various ☼ ◗ M Ct Ay

Foliage. Trailing plants with green or pink and green striped foliage and tiny, three-petaled flowers. Easy to root and fast-growing but not frost-hardy.

HERBACEOUS PERENNIALS AND ALPINES

ACAENA
❋ ◑ 6 inches ☼ D SdCt Ay

New Zealand burr. Foliage. Green, khaki or blue-gray. Useful but invasive groundcover or trailers, forming thick mats of interwoven stems clothed with masses of pinnate leaves and insignificant, tufty flowers in summer. *Acaena caesiiglauca* has gray-blue foliage, "Copper Carpet" has bronze foliage and cream flowers, and *A. adscendens*, also blue-leaved, will sometimes climb, but needs support.

ACONITUM
❋ ⚭ 3 feet ◗ M SdDv Su

Monkshood. Flowers. Blue. Tough genus for cool sites with deeply cut foliage and spires of blue, blue and white or cream hooded flowers. *A. napellus* blooms in summer, *A. carmichaelii* in the fall. The climbing *A. volubile* is a useful fall-flowering plant to plait into a living screen. Highly poisonous.

ALYSSUM
❋ ♥ 6 inches ☼ D M Sd SpSu

Flowers. White, yellow. The annual kinds (*Alyssum maritima* – more correctly *Lobularia maritima*) are used for edging or bedding and are usually white. "Snowdrift" is a popular strain. *A. saxatile* is a good container subject.

ANIGOZANTHOS
❋ ⚭ 2 feet ☼ D <pH7 DvSd Su

Kangaroo paw. Flowers. Red/green. Tufts of sword-shaped foliage and strange, furry, tubular flowers produced on sprays. *A. manglesii* is red in bud opening to green. *A. flavida* is light green.

ANTHEMIS
❋ ⚭ ◑ various ☼ D DvSd SuFa

Dog fennel. Flowers, foliage. White and yellow. Feathery or filigree foliage, often with a distinctive aroma, and daisy flowers, usually single, white with yellow centers. *A. cretica* subsp. *cupaniana* drapes gracefully over container sides, and produces white daisies for months in spring and summer. For Chamomile (*Anthemis nobile*) see under its current botanical name *Chamaemelum nobile*.

ANTIRRHINUM
❋ ♥ 2 feet ☼ D M Sd Su

Snapdragon. Flowers. All colors. Short-lived perennials mostly bred from *A. majus*. All are suitable for containers and good varieties include "Coronette" in red, orange, pink and yellow, and the dwarf "Princess" series. There are also strains with open-ended flowers, such as "Little Darling."

ARGYRANTHEMUM FRUTESCENS
⚑ ⬇ 3 feet ☼ DM CtSd Su

Marguerite. Flowers. White, pink, yellow. Shrubby plants with aromatic, lobed leaves and flowers from early summer to late fall. The species is white with a yellow center, but "Mary Wootton" is a pale pink double and "Jamaica Primrose" pale yellow with darker centers. Best if pinched back frequently to encourage bushy growth.

AUBRIETA
✳ ⬥ 6 inches ☼ D CtSd Sp

Flowers. Purple, pink, rosy red. Popular rock plants which trail over the sides of containers and are smothered with blooms in spring. The foliage is evergreen but needs trimming hard back after flowering to prevent straggly growth. Many cultivars available including "Argenteo-variegata" with silver leaf margins and "Joy," a purple semi-double.

BEGONIA
⚑ ⬠ various CtSd

Outdoor groups can be classified as follows.
Semperflorens Small, bushy plants with fleshy leaves and a long succession of mainly pink double or single flowers. Varieties include mixes, such as "Party Fun" with bronze leaves, and single colors, such as "Coco Bright Scarlet." "Pink Avalanche" is ideal for hanging baskets.
Tuberous Derived from *B.* x *tuberhybrida* and including huge-flowered show plants like "Can Can" (peach), "Midas" (yellow) or "Apricot Cascade." The "Nonstop" strain comes in a mix of vibrant colors.
Species Examples include *B. sutherlandii*, with copper-orange blooms carried on pendulous stems, and cane-stemmed begonias, such as *B. coccinea* (Angelwing).

OPPOSITE *Antirrhinums come in a full range of heights and colors, and flower all summer.*

CAMPANULA ISOPHYLLA
⚑ ⬥ 6 inches ☼ DM CtSd SuFa

Bellflower. Flowers. Blue or white. The trailing habit, evergreen foliage, beauty of its saucer-shaped flowers and long-flowering season make this a super subject for hanging baskets or any other container that lets it trail.

CENTRANTHUS
✳ ⚘ 2½ feet ☼ D Sd Sp Su

Red valerian. Flowers. Red, pink or white. Useful perennials which can thrive in the harshest conditions, providing cool, glaucous foliage and months of colorful flowers produced on misty sprays. They will even colonize old walls, without causing them any damage. The pink is a poor color, but the brick-red and white forms are certainly well worth seeking.

CHEIRANTHUS
⚑ ⚘ various ☼ D SdCt Sp

Wallflower. Flowers. Mauve, purple, ivory, orange, red, yellow. Bedding wallflowers, not hardy in sustained frost, make perfect companions for spring bulbs. Perennial forms are good in containers, and include the strongly fragrant double yellow "Harpur Crewe" and the purple "Chelsea Jacket."

CHRYSANTHEMUM (SYN. DENDRANTHEMA)
✳ ⚑ various ☼ DM CtSd SuFa

A huge genus of florist's plants, many of which make fine container subjects. The most durable outdoor types are spray varieties. "Korean" chrysanthemums are especially durable in the fall, and the new cushion chrysanthemums show promise. The Japanese variety "Mei-Kyo" is far from new but its plummy pink button flowers, that come out in late fall, always delight and guarantee color in the garden toward the end of the year.

● shade | D dry | M moist | <pH7 needs acid soil | Sd seed | Ct cuttings | Dv division

COLEUS
⌂ ❦ various ○ M CtSd Su

Flame nettle. Foliage. Red, bronze, cream. The vivid coloring of the nettle-like leaves makes this a valuable plant for a frost-free site or as temporary summer bedding.

DAHLIA
❉ ❦ various ○ M DvCtSd Su

Flowers. Huge genus with flowers of almost every color. Tubers must be stored frost-free. There are three main flower types.
Pompon Rounded, button flowers. Examples: "Whale's Rhonda" (purple red); "Small World" (white); "Willo's Violet."
Cactus Narrow, tubular petals, open flowers. Examples: "Paul Chester" (orange); "White Klankstad."
Decorative Large, broad-petaled flowers. Examples: "Ruby Wedding;" "Hamari Gold" (bronze).

There are many other forms. "Bedding" dahlias, such as "Redskin" (dark foliage, variously colored flowers), are usually grown each year from seed.

DIANTHUS
❉ ❦ 8 inches ○ D CtSd Su

Pink, carnation. Flowers, fragrance. Pink, salmon, red, yellow, cream, white. Showy, often strongly scented flowers, many plumed or ruffled, which are set off by blue-gray foliage. For containers, border pinks are especially good and repeating varieties, such as "Doris" (salmon and carmine) or "Diane" (salmon to apricot), are the best value. Old pink varieties such as "Dad's Favorite" (white and crimson) and "Mrs. Sinkins" (white) have the best scent.

HAKONECHLOA MACRA "AUREOLA"
❉ 18 inches ○ ◗ M CtDv SpSu

Foliage. Graceful grass with arching gold and green striped leaves and rust flowers.

ABOVE Hosta sieboldiana *is just one of several hostas which thrive in containers.*

HELIOTROPIUM
⌂ ❦ 2 feet+ ○ D CtSd Su

Cherry pie. Flowers, fragrance. Purple. Deeply veined, dark foliage topped by sprays of dark purple, fragrant flowers all summer.

HELXINE SOLEIROLII (SYN. SOLEIROLIA SOLEIROLII)
⌂ ↕ 3 inches ● ◗ M Dv Ay

Mind-your-own-business. Foliage. Invasive, mat-forming perennial forming a network of stems with tiny green leaves. Useful to cover bare patches but can become troublesome.

HOSTA
❉ ❦ various ● ◗ ○ M Dv SpSu

Plantain lily. Foliage, flowers. Mauve. Broad foliage emerges from ground level in spring and, in some species, can reach 12 inches or more in height. Most species have pretty lilac to mauve flowers in summer. Good species include *H. sieboldiana* (blue-gray leaves), *H. undulata* "Albomarginata" ("Thomas Hogg") (green-white variegations), "Gold Standard" and the diminutive "Gold Edger."

❉ hardy | ❦ slightly tender | ⌂ tender | ↕ erect | ↕ trailing | ❦ bushy | ○ sun | ◗ partial shade

ABOVE *Modern garden forms of* Impatiens *have the advantage of bright flower colors, and a long and abundant flowering season. This plant is blooming well in relatively dense shade – another useful attribute enjoyed by members of the balsam family.*

IMPATIENS
⊢ 12 inches ● ◗ M SdCt Su

Balsam, busy Lizzie. Flowers. Most colors. Valuable groups of half-hardy perennials which flower well in gloomy conditions. New strains are constantly being developed. Reliable series include Duet, Novette and Super Elfin, all of which come in color mixtures, but many are also available in single colors.

LOBELIA
⊢ ❈ various M SdDvCt Su

Flowers. Blue, purple, red. Large genus of perennials, some like *L. cardinalis,* growing tall with coppery leaves and blood-red flowers. The familiar, 8-inch, blue *L. erinus is* probably the most popular container plant in the world. Although deep blue is the commonest color, there are many color strains, including "Cambridge Blue" (light blue), "Color Cascade" (mixed blue, pink, purple) and "Crystal Palace" (dark blue, bronzed foliage).

MELIANTHUS MAJOR
⌂ ↓ 6 feet ○ ◗ M Ct Su

Honeybush. Foliage. Shapely gray-green, toothed leaflets produced abundantly in warm, moist conditions. Not at all dependable in cold climates.

ORIGANUM
❈ ⊢ ♀ various ○ D SdCt SuFa

Oregano, marjoram. Foliage, flavoring. The pot herb is *O. vulgare,* but ornamental species of great beauty include *O. laevigatum,* with purple flowers and mahogany bracts, and *O. rotundifolium,* apple-green flushed pink flowers looking like little hops.

PELARGONIUM
⌂ various ○ D CtSd SpSuFa

Geranium. Flowers, foliage. The mainstay of most container gardens, these African natives have been popular since the early nineteenth century. Every species and hybrid is suitable for container use. Limited space prevents much detail but groups are roughly categorized as follows.

Scented foliage Examples: *P. capitatum* (like roses); *P. crispum* (lemony); *P. tomentosum* (minty); *P. quercifolium* (musky).

Zonal The traditional geraniums with red, pink or white flowers and rounded leaves, often marked with concentric coloring. Examples: "Dale Queen" (salmon pink); "Dolly Varden" (red with cream zoning on leaf); "Orange Ricard."

Regal Leaves plain green, serrated and trumpet-shaped flowers in purple, pink or lavender shades. Examples: "Autumn Festival" (salmon, white throat); "Manx Maid" (pink with red veins); "Purple Emperor."

Ivy-leaved Trailing plants with hairless foliage and many colorful flowers. Examples: "L'Elegante" (cream variegated foliage, lilac flowers); "Mini Cascade" (red); "Amethyst" (light mauve); "Barbe Bleu" (deep purple to crimson).

● shade │ D dry │ M moist │ <pH7 needs acid soil │ Sd seed │ Ct cuttings │ Dv division

PENSTEMON
⚘ ❦ various ☉ ◗ M CtSd SuFa

Flowers. Red, pink, purple, blue. North American natives with tubular flowers carried on self-supporting stems. Most good hybrids are repeat-flowering but susceptible to frost. Examples: "Garnet" (red); "Alice Hindley" (lavender and white); "Sour Grapes" (green and purple); "Apple Blossom" (pink and white); "Evelyn" (pink).

PETUNIA
⌂ ❦ 12 inches ☉ D Sd Su

Flowers. All colors. Vastly popular plants for containers. A summer-long succession of floppy, saucer-shaped flowers is produced on plants whose foliage is slightly glutinous. Hot, dry weather suits petunias. New strains arrive every year, and current favorites include "Mirage" and "Joy Multiflora." The nearest to a yellow flower so far is "Brass Band."

PHYGELIUS
⚘ ✳ ❦ 3 feet + ☉ M CtDv Su

Flowers. Red, salmon, yellow. Shrubs best treated as perennials and cut back every spring. Vigorous stems, tubular flowers. *P. aequalis* (pinkish salmon) and its cultivar "Yellow Trumpet" are pick of the bunch.

SAXIFRAGA
✳ ❦ various ☉ ◗ DM CtSdDv Ay

Saxifrage. Flowers, foliage. Large and variable genus of mainly rock plants. Easiest is *S.* x *urbium* or London pride, which is evergreen with sprays of pink flowers in late spring. Cushion saxifrages are good in tufa. Aizöon species produce large sprays of bloom from neat rosettes of foliage.

STACHYS BYZANTINA
✳ ⬍ 12 inches ☉ DM CtDv Ay

Foliage. Felty leaves on low-growing plants which form a dense cover. The flower spikes are also thickly clothed, concealing the dull red blooms.

VERBENA
⚘ ✳ various ☉ DM SdCtDv Su

Flowers. Red, pink, blue, white. Colorful tender perennials which produce successions of flowers throughout summer. *V. bonariensis* is a tall species, growing to 6 feet, but most verbenas stay below 12 inches. *V. peruviana* has umbels of brilliant red flowers, and the cultivars of *V.* x *hybrida* have a bright color range. "Sissinghurst" is a fine, pink, near-hardy perennial.

VIOLA
✳ ⚘ various ☉ M DvSd Ct Ay

Flowers, fragrance. Most colors except red. Pansies and garden violas provide year-round color. The best winter pansies are the "Universal" strain. Sweet violets, *V. odorata*, provide spring scent, and the double Parma violets have double the fragrance. Summer species include long-lasting *V. cornuta* mostly blue, violet or white. Cut hard back several times a season for more flowers.

✳ hardy | ⚘ slightly tender | ⌂ tender | ⬍ erect | ⬍ trailing | ❦ bushy | ☉ sun | ◗ partial shade

ANNUALS

BRACHYCOME IBERIDIFOLIA
❄ ♀ 18 inches ☿ DM Sd Su

Swan river daisy. Flowers. Blue, pinkish. Scented daisy flowers on stems which are lax enough to allow them to hang gracefully over the sides of a container but not to collapse.

CALENDULA
❄ ♀ 12 inches ☿ DM Sd Su

Pot marigold. Flowers. Orange, yellow, lemon. Aromatic green foliage and large blooms with petals arranged in rays. The first flowers appear in late winter but plants stay colorful right through until the end of summer, especially if dead flowers are pulled off. Easily grown from seed sown directly into containers. Many "improved" strains are available but the new are no better than the old. "Art Shades" has vigor, and a fine range of color from deep orange to pale yellow.

CAPSICUM
❄ ♪ 3 feet ☿ DM Sd SuFa

Ornamental pepper. Fruit. Green changing to red or yellow. Although varieties like "Holiday Cheer" are primarily ornamental, most other members of the tomato family, which includes eggplants, sweet bell peppers, chilies and pimientos, are decorative and useful.

ABOVE *The Swan river daisy,* Brachycome iberidifolia, *is a tender annual with plenty of flower power. The lax stems should be pinched back at first to encourage thick, bushy growth. Good well-drained soil and full sun are essential for maximum color.*

ONOPORDON
❄ ♪ 8 feet ☿ D Sd SpSu

Giant thistle. Foliage. A monster plant with silver, felty foliage, vicious spikes and, in its second year, huge sprays of lilac-mauve thistle flowers. Definitely not for the small garden.

RESEDA ODORATA
❄ ♪ 2 feet ☿ M Sd Su

Mignonette. Fragrance. Unexciting, green-tinged flowers with orange stamens but sweetly fragrant and irresistible to bees.

SOLANUM CAPSICASTRUM
◠ ♀ 12 inches ☿ M Sd Wi

Winter cherry. Fruit. A decorative member of the tomato family with deep green foliage, little white and orange flowers and oblong orange-scarlet fruits.

● shade │ D dry │ M moist │ <pH7 needs acid soil │ Sd seed │ Ct cuttings │ Dv division

BULBS, CORMS AND TUBERS

AGAPANTHUS
✳ ⌂ ⬍ 3 feet ○ D SdDv Su

African lily. Flowers. Blue, white. Strap-like foliage and stiff flower stems topped with generous umbels of many soft blue flowers. Fine examples include "Headbourne Hybrids," blue and fairly hardy, and *A. inapertus*, which grows large, with generous umbels.

ALLIUM
✳ ⬍ various ○ D SdDv SpSu

Garlic, onion, etc. Flower, foliage, culinary. A vast genus of valuable and beautiful plants which are easy to grow, with colors ranging from purple, mauve, blue, pink to pure white. Many have a pungent odor. Chives, *A. schoenoprasum*, and garlic chives, *A. nigrum*, combine utility with beauty. *A. aflatunense*, *A. giganteum* and *A. christophii* all have superb purple flower heads in early summer. Yellow garlics include *A. moly* and *A. flavum*. The tiny *A. oreophilum* (syn. *A. ostrowskianum*) glows like a ruby. *A. karataviense* has decorative broad, purplish leaves in spring.

ANEMONE
✳ ⬍ various ○ D SdDv SpSu

Windflower. Flowers. Red, blue, yellow, pink, white. All sizes from the 6-inch *A. appenina*, which flowers in spring, to the fall-blooming, 4-foot *A.* x *hybrida* "Honorine Jobert." Florist's anemones "St. Brigid" (double) and "de Caen" (single) series are fine in containers as are *A. blanda* (blue, pink and white) and *A.* x *fulgens* (red).

CROCUS
✳ ⬍ 4 inches ○ D SdDv SpWiFa

Flowers. Yellow, blue, white. A large genus of hardy winter, spring and fall blooms. Dutch hybrids grow big and come in yellow, deep blue, white or striped varieties. Fall species include *C. speciosus* and *C. kotschyanus* subsp. *kotschyanus* (syn. *C. zonatus*), both lavender-purple shades. Winter species of crocus include *C. ancyrensis* (orange yellow), *C. imperati* (beige and lavender) and the many *C. chrysanthus* cultivars (yellow, cream, bronze and violet).

✳ hardy | ✶ slightly tender | ⌂ tender | ⬍ erect | ⬊ trailing | ♣ bushy | ○ sun | ◗ partial shade

CYCLAMEN, HARDY
✳ ◖ 4 inches ☼ ◗ D Sd FaSp

Flowers, foliage. Pink, white. Frost-proof species include the fall-flowering *C. hederifolium* and the winter-flowering *C. coum.* Prolonged, deep frost will eventually kill these plants.

GLADIOLUS
✳ ◖ various ☼ D DvSd SuFa

Sword lily. Flowers. Most colors except blue. A huge range of cultivars from the petite "Primulinus" varieties to the monstrous show forms. Fine varieties include "The Bride," the soft yellow *G. natalensis* var. *primulinus* and fall-flowering *G. papilio* (syn. *G. purpureoauratus),* which is mushroom-colored, greenish and yellow with hooded flowers.

LILIUM
✳ ⵢ various ☼ ◗ M SdDv SuFa

Lily. Flowers, fragrance. Huge genus with many useful container subjects. Humus-rich compost is essential and regular feeding beneficial. The large, late-flowering lilies like *L. speciosum* (white), *L. auratum* (white and pink) and *L. regale* (white) and their hybrids (many shades) are especially suitable.

MUSCARI
✳ ◖ 6 inches ☼ D DvSd Sp

Grape hyacinth. Flowers. Blue. Low-growing, early-flowering plants with spikes of small, rounded flowers. *M. botryoides, M. armeniacum* and *M. comosum* are all easy to grow. The closely related chionodoxa and scilla also provide valuable early color, and will multiply to form colonies.

OPPOSITE LEFT *This agapanthus is a vigorous, free-flowering garden hybrid.*

OPPOSITE RIGHT Allium karataviense *is one of many useful ornamental onions.*

NARCISSUS
✳ ◖ various ☼ ◗ MD DvSd Sp

Daffodil, narcissus, jonquil. Flowers, fragrance. Yellow, white. White narcissus do especially well in containers and lend themselves to forcing. Some of the larger daffodils have a messy aftermath of foliage, but early hybrids such as "February Gold" and "Peeping Tom" (yellow) and late jonquils like "Bobbysoxer" (yellow) are neater in habit.

TULIPA
✳ ◖ various ☼ D Dv Sp

Tulip. Flowers. Red, yellow, orange, pink, cream, white. All tulips are happy in containers. Dwarf doubles, giant "breeder" tulips, lily-flowered hybrids and most of the wild species provide bold splashes of color in spring. Of species, *T. greigii* and *T. kaufmanniana* provide some of the brightest blooms.

BELOW *Of all cyclamen species,* C. persicum *has the best scent and the most shapely flowers, but it is not frost-hardy.*

INDEX

Page numbers in *italics* refer to illustrations.

Abutilon 110, 142, 143
Acaena 150
Acer (Maple) 26, 66, 109, 143, *143*
Aconitum 21, 81, 150
Agapanthus 56–7, 137, 156, *156*
Allium 39, 156, *156*
Aloysia triphylla 87
Alpines 44, *45,* 46, 48, *48,* 49, 66, *90,* 104–5, *106, 122,* 129, 150–4
Alyssum 24, 150
Amaryllis 113
Ampelopsis 35, 78
Anemone 48, *94,* 156
Anigozanthos 150
Annuals 119, 129, 155
Anthemis 72, 150
Antirrhinum 26, 150, *150*
Arbors 10, 11, *80,* 91, 130
Argyranthemum frutescens 151
Artemisia *17, 45,* 100, *146*
Arum-lily 24, *35*
Asarina erubescens 81
Aspect of site 15, 22–7, 39, 105
Asplenium 49
Aubrieta 151
Aucuba japonica 27
Azalea 20, *22, 36,* 53, *102,* 123, 132, 146

Balconies 52, 57, 62, *62, 63,* 76
balcony boxes 50–1, *51,* 125
Begonia 20, 24, 42, 151
Berberis 20
Betula 51, 143
Bluebell, California *116*
Bonsai 108–9, *108–9*
Bougainvillea 20, 51, 66, 78
Box, clipped 81, 132
Box elder 143
Brachycome iberidifolia 155, *155*
Buddleia 20, 21
Bulbs, corms and tubers *19,* 25, 27, 42, 48, 114–16, *114,* 126, *126,* 137, 156–7

Cactus 27, 66, 95
Calcifuges 102–3, *102,* 123
Calendula (Pot marigold) 20, 155
Calluna 143
Camellia 53, 102, 143
Campanula isophylla 21, 54, 151

Canary creeper *101*
Capsicum 155
Carex flagellifera 42
Caryopteris x *clandonensis* 21
Centranthus 151
Ceratostigma willmottianum 21
Ceterach officinarum 49
Chaenomeles 20, 109, 130, 144
Chamaecyparis 21
Chamaemelum nobile 150
Chamomile 72
Chilies 100, 155
Chionodoxa 157
Choisya 21, 144, *144*
Chrysanthemum 20, 21, 137, 151
Cineraria 116
Cistus 15, 70, 144
Citrus 22, *85,* 144
Clematis 24, 53, 78, 104–5, 120, 126, 130, 147
Clerondendrum trichotomum 21
Climbers 12, 13, 15, *18,* 24, 39, 51, 56–7, 62, 67, 71, *73,* 76, 78–81, *79,* 82, *110,* 134, 147–9
training and pruning *118–19,* 119, 130, *132*
Coleus 151
Color 11–12, 16–21, 25, 51, 68, *70,* 74, 75, 76, 94–5, 98, 100, *104*
grouping plants 13, 76, 81, 90
vegetables 82, *83,* 84
Composts 7, 41, 46, 65, 102, 122–3, *124,* 125, 129
Conifers 21, 26, 47, *133*
Conservatories 89, 110–13, *110–12*
Containers 24, 28–55, *28–55,* 59, *59,* 60–1, *61,* 65, 66, 69, 74, 88–113, *92,* 120, *121,* 146
capacity 29, 36, 120
weathered 7, *28–9, 33, 45, 48,* 60–1
Convolvulus 26, 144, 147, *147*
Cordyline 75
Cornus alba 20
Cosmos atrosanguineus 137
Cotton thistle 68
Covers and cloches *104–7,* 105–7
Crinum 137
Crocus 21, 42, 48, *126,* 156
Cryptomeria japonica 109
Cyclamen 48–9, *103,* 157
Cypress 81, *90, 108*
Cytisus 75

Daffodil 116, *126,* 137, 157
Dahlia *17, 25,* 79, *83,* 100, 137, 152
Daisy 88–9
Daisy bush *80*
Daphne collina 47
Delphinium 104–5
Dendranthema 20, 21, 137, 151
Design 10–15, 66–73, 89
Dianthus 152
Diascia 35, 49
Dionaea muscipula 107
Diseases and disorders 25, 104, 107, 116, 123, 124, 128, 136, 138–9
Dorycnium hirsutum 144
Drainage 29, *33,* 36, 46, 54, 65, 72, 90–1, 104, *123,* 124–5, *124*

Eccremocarpus scaber 81, 147
Echeveria *15,* 47, 66, 72, 120
Erica (Heather) 144
Eucalyptus 144
Eucomis 123
Evergreens *10, 19,* 22, 25, 26, 27, *27,* 47, *61,* 74, *75,* 81, 114, 143–6
Exacum affine 32

Feeding 40, 42, 45, 66, 102, 125, 128–9
Ferns 22, 24, 25, 39, 45, 49, 62, 96, 116
Fertilizers 40, 82, 102, 122, 123
Ficus (Fig) 25, 84, *105,* 145
Foliage 11–12, 13, 25, 39, 47, *52,* 76, 90, 98
discoloration 104, 123, 124, 128, 139
Food plants 57, 58, 66, 82–7, 100–1, 129, *139*
Forget-me-not *17, 19,* 21, 42, 116
Formal designs 10–11, 68, 74, 81, 89, *94,* 94, 96, 97, 99
Forsythia 20, 47
Fremontodendron 14, 130
Frost 27, 52, 78, 120, 137
Fruit 57, 58, *64,* 66, 82, 84–6, 109, 129, 145, 146
Fuchsia 14, *35,* 42, 75, *75,* 79, 100

Galanthus reginae-olgae 48
Gardening techniques 119–139
Garrya elliptica 130
Gentian 48, 53, 102

Gentiana asclepiadea 21
Geranium 21, *44*
see also Pelargonium
Gladiolus 137, 157
Glechoma hederacea 33, 147
Grape hyacinth see *Muscari*
Grasses 33, 42, 98
Greenhouses 108, 110, 134, *134,* 137
Grouping plants 13–14, 76, 81, 90

Hakonechloa 33, 42, 98, 152
Hanging baskets 40–3, *40–3,* 84, 95
Heathers 102, 143, 144
Hedera (Ivy) 22, 24, 39, 42, 45, 74, *104,* 130, *130, 133,* 147
Hedges 60, 81, 91, 92, *92,* 94
clipping 119, 132
Helichrysum 26, 39, 42, *50,* 100, *101*
Heliotropium 39, 100, 152
Helxine soleirolii 72, 152
Herbaceous plants 20, 21, 25, 114, 150–4
Herbs 39, 72, 86–7, *86–7, 95,* 100
see also *Origanum*
Hippeastrum aulicum 113
Holly see *Ilex*
Hollyhock *53*
Honesty 24
Honeysuckle see *Lonicera*
Hosta *11,* 22, 24, 33, 58, 67, 98, 152, *152*
Hyacinth 21, 24, 25, 55, 116
Hydrangea 11, *23,* 70, 78, *120,* 130, 145, *145*

Iberis 126
Ilex (Holly) 20, 21, 25, 47, 81, 109, 120, 132
Impatiens (Busy Lizzie) *13, 17,* 21, 22, 27, *31,* 39, *73, 75,* 76, 92, 153, *153*
Informal designs 10, 11, 68, 81
Ipomoea 78, 147
Iris 20, *126*
Ivy see *Hedera*
Ivy, Ground 33, 147

Jasminum (Jasmine) 78, 148
Jekyll, Gertrude 13, 51
Juniper *36,* 47, 109

Kalanchoe blossfeldiana 136
Kniphofia "Percy's Pride" 21

Lantana *17*, 24
Lapageria 53, 78, 148
Lathyrus 21, *36*, 148
Laurel 27, 145
Laurus nobilis (Bay) 22, 25, *94*, *99*, 110, 132, 145
Lavandula (Lavender) *86*, 87, 100, 145
Lavatera 145
Lemon balm 14
Lilium 69, *70*, 102, 157
Lily-of-the-valley 25
Lobelia 39, *41*, 42, 54, *83*, 153
Lobularia maritima 150
London pride 25, 154
Lonicera (Honeysuckle) *53*, 78, 126, 130, 148

Maidenhair fern 116
Maidenhair spleenwort 49
Malcolmia maritima 126
Marigold, Pot (Calendula) 20, 155
Maurandya erubescens 81
Melianthus major 90, 153
Melissa officinalis 14
Mentha pulegium 86
Metasequoia glyptostroboides 109
Mixed planting 30, 120
Moss 45, 107, 122–3, 134, *135*
  for hanging baskets 41, 42
Muscari *31*, 157
Myrtle 22, 110

Narcissus 21, 24, 25, 48, *127*, 157
  see also Daffodil
Nasturtium *see Tropaeolum*
Nicotiana *13*, *90*

Onopordon 68, 155
Orchids 62, 76
Origanum 12, 39, 42, 86, 153
Overwintering 7, *35*, 110, 120, 137

Pansy *17*, *33*, *75*, *83*, 116, *154*
Pansy, winter 20, *37*, 42, 154
Papaver somniferum 68, *70*, *127*
Parthenocissus *73*, 74, 130
Passiflora 110, *132*, 148, *148*
Paths 71, 92–4, *112*
Patios 89, 97–100
Pelargonium 24, 26, *37*, 39, *40*, *65*, *75*, *83*, 87, 95, 100, *111*, *115*, 153
Pepper 100, 101, 129, 155
Periwinkle 149, *149*
Pesticides, for food crops 82

Pests 25, 101, 138–9
Petunia 20, 21, 26, *31*, 42, *75*, *99*, *101*, 154
Phacelia campanularia 116
Philadelphus 21
Phlox "Chattahoochee" *8–9*
Phygelius *13*, 22, 154
Picea glauca 21, 26
Pitcher plant 107
Planting 126, *127*
Plectranthus coleoides 33
Plumbago *18*, 22, 24, *52*
Polygonum baldschuanicum 78
Poppy 68, *70*, 102, *127*
Primrose 20, 116
Primula 20, 49, 53, 102, 107
Propagation 15, *106*, 123, 126, 134–6, *134*, *136*
  see also Overwintering
Pruning and training 66, *66*, *109*, *118–19*, 119, 130–4
Prunus 109, 145
Pulmonaria saccharata 21
Punica granatum 146

Quince, Japanese 130, 144

Raised beds 11, 52–3, *53*, 60
Reseda odorata 39, 155
Rhodochiton atrosanguineum *12*, 148
Rhododendron 20, 21, 24, *74*, 102, 120, 123, 132, 146
Ribes sanguineum 20
Robinia 146
Rock cress 25
Rodgersia 25
Roof gardens 57, *58*, 59, 61, *64*, 64–73, *65*
Roots 58–60, 66, 120, 122, *123*, 126, 134–5, *136*, 137
Rosa (Rose) 20, 21, 24, *58*, *61*, *67*, *70*, 78, 100, *121*, 129, 138, 146, *146*, 148, 149
  climbing 53, *58*, 71, 78, 149
Rubus phoenicolasius *44*
Rustyback 49

Salix 19, 27, 47, 109, 146
Salvia patens 24, 137
Santolina 146
Sarracenia 107
Saxifraga 25, 48, 49, *75*, 154
Scent and aroma 12, 25, 39, 47, 51, 53, 87, 100
Schizophragma 81
Schizostylis coccinea "Alba" 21
Scilla 157

Screens (of plants) 15, 24, 61, 62, 71, *73*, 81, *81*, 82, *83*, 92
Seakale 107
Seasonal effect 40, 42, 68, *70*, 90, 114–17
Sedge 42, 122
Sedum 25, 26, *45*, 47, *55*, *56–7*, 66
Sempervivum 47, *54*, *55*, 66, 72
Senecio 100
Shaded aspect 15, 22–5, 39, 52, 57, 58, 62, 66, 76, *76*, 105, *105*
Shasta daisy *70*
Shrubs 11, 20, 21, 32, 46, 47, 91, 95, 114, 129, 134–5, 143–6
  in balcony boxes 51
  in contained gardens 58, 62, *70*, *75*, 87
  pruning *118–19*, 119, 130–3
Silver foliage *17*, 19, 21, *45*, 100, 107, 109, 144, *146*
Sinks *see* Troughs and sinks
Snowdrop 48
Soft fruit 84–5
  see also Strawberry
Soil 12–13, 22, *26*, 26–7, 46–7, 52, 53, 57, *61*, 90–1, 102–5, 122–3, *123*, 124, 140–157
Solanum capsicastrum 116, 155
Soleirolia soleirolii 72, 152
Sorbus cashmiriana 21, 53
Stachys 14, *93*, 154
Steps and stairs 10, 11, *76–7*
Stock, Virginian 126
Stonecrop, Biting *26*
Strawberry 58, 84–6, *84*, 101, 107, 129
Succulents 27
Sundew 107
Swan river daisy 155, *155*
Sweetpea *36*, 148

Tagetes (Marigold) 20, 25, *56–7*, *69*, 101, 138, *139*
Tamarisk 75
Terraces 11, 74–5, 89, *96*, 97–100, 110
Thistle, Cotton 68
Thunbergia alata 26
Tigridia 137
Tomato 82, 100, 101, *101*, 129, 138, *139*, 155
Topiary 77, 81, *94*, 119, *130–1*, 132–3
Tradescantia 149
Trailers and danglers 33, 39, 40, *40*, *69*, 74, 76, 86, 147–9

Trees 11–12, *14*, 22, 25, 26, 32, 46, 47, 51, 58, 60, 61, 62, *64*, 66, 67, *67*, *118–19*, 129, 130–5, 143–6
Trellises 62, 71, 79, 81, 130
Tropaeolum (Nasturtium) *18*, 20, 25, 42, *75*, *140–1*, 149
Troughs and sinks 44–9, *44–9*
Tubs and pots 30–5, 60, *61*
Tufa 44, 49, *49*
Tulipa (Tulip) *19*, 20, 21, 24, *114*, 116, 126, *126*, 137,157

Urns *17*, 33, *35*, 74, *94*, 101, 120

Valerian, Red 151
Vegetables 57, 58, 61, 66, 82, *83*, 84, 100–1, *101*, 104, 107, 129, 155, 156
Venus's flytrap 107
Verbena *17*, *91*, 154
Veronica gentianoides 17
Vertical gardening 53, 57, 78–81, *79*, *80*, *81*
Viburnum 21, *117*
Vinca 149, *149*
Viola *33*, 116, 154, *154*
Violet, Sweet 24, 39, 154
Vista stops 71, *73*, 91–5, *94*
Vitis (Vine) 15, 78, *80*, 84, 149

Wallflower 20, 24, 42, 116, 151
Walls 10, 11, 39, *43*, 62, 78–81, *81*, 130
Water features 52, *69*, 72, *96*, 96–7
Watering 15, 25, 45, 46–7, 50, 65, 95, 104, 107, 120, 122, 123, 124–5, *124*
  hanging baskets 40, 42
  roof gardens 66
White plants *17*, 21, 22–4, 25, 53, *104*
Willow *see Salix*
Wind 15, 27, 32, 40–1, 50, 54, 57, 66, 95, 105, 120, 122
Windbreaks 15, 61, 105
Window boxes 36–9, *36*, *38*, 116, 125
Wineberry *44*
Winter storage 7, *35*, 110, 120, 137
Wisteria *43*, 78, 149

Zantedeschia aethiopica 24
Zebrina 149

ACKNOWLEDGMENTS

Marijke Heuff and the publisher would like to thank the following for allowing us to photograph in their gardens:

1 The Priona Gardens; 2 Nursery Overhagen; 5 designer Els Proost; 5 left Mr & Mrs Kloeg-Ammerlaan; 5 right Mr J van den Brink; 6–7 Quinta do Palheiro Ferrairo; 8–9 Mr & Mrs Merton, The Old Rectory; 10 left Mr & Mrs Brinkworth; 10 right Walda Pairon Giardini; 11 Mrs L Goossenaerts-Miedema; 12 above Nursery de Kleine Plantage; 12 below Mr & Mrs van Wijk-Mijnlief; 13 above The Priona Gardens; 15 below Nursery Overhagen; 14 left The Priona Gardens; 14 right de Rhulenhof Nursery and Gardens; 15 Mr & Mrs Groenewegen-Groot; 16 Gardens Mien Ruys; 16–17 Mr & Mrs ter Kuile-Nijpels; 17 above Nursery Overhagen; 17 below Mr & Mrs Merton, The Old Rectory; 18 left Mr and Mrs Helsen-Buurman; 18 right Ton ter Linden; 19 left Gardens Mien Ruys; 19 right Wala Pairon Giardini; 22 Mr & Mrs Helsen-Buurman; 23 Mr & Mrs Degeyter; 24 Mr O Hoek; 25 Mr & Mrs Degeyter; 26 de Rhulenhof Nursery and Gardens; 28–29 Mrs L Goossenaerts-Miedema; 30 Mr & Mrs Mariée-Jansen; 31 above left Gardens Mien Ruys; 31 below left Gardens Mien Ruys; 31 above right Walenburg; 31 below right The Priona Gardens; 32 Ineke Greve; 33 above Mr & Mrs Lambooy-Raats; 33 below Mr & Mrs ter Kuile-Nijpels; 34 Nursery Overhagen; 35 above Mr L J Ph Groeneveld; 35 below left de Rhuenhof Nursery and Gardens; 35 below right Nursery de Kleine Plantage; 36 above designer Hannah Moser; 41 left Mr & Mrs P Benbridge, Flopsy Cottage; 41 right Mr & Mrs P Benbridge, Flopsy Cottage; 44 Mrs M van Bennekom-Scheffer; 45 Mr & Mrs Michielsen-van Pelt; 46–47 Mrs Anthony Biddulph; 48 Major & Mrs Mordaunt-Hare, Fitzhouse; 49 Mr & Mrs Merton, The Old Rectory; 51 Mr D Burgess; 52 Patricia van Roosmalen; 53 above architect John Burgee, garden Gwen Burgee with Tim du Val; 53 below Marijke Heuff; 55 above left Mrs M van Bennekom-Scheffer; 58 left garden designed, developed and maintained by Val Gerry; 59 Mr & Mrs Langendijk-Egger; 60–61 Ineke Greve; 61 garden designed, developed and maintained by Val Gerry; 62 Maggier Geiger, The Window Box; 63 designer Ada Roest; 64 Maggie Geiger, The Window Box; 65 above Sigurd Ludke; 65 below garden designed, developed and maintained by Val Gerry; 67 left Dr Z Lothane; 67 right garden designed, developed and maintained by Val Gerry; 68–69 Maggie Geiger, The Window Box; 69 above garden designed, developed and maintained by Val Gerry; 68–69 Maggie Geiger, The Window Box; 69 above garden designed, developed and maintained by Val Gerry; 70 Mr & Mrs Langendijk-Egger; 70–71 garden designed, developed and maintained by Val Gerry; 72 Dr Z Lothane; 73 designer Tim Du Val; 74 right Mr & Mrs Gerritsen-Buurman; 74 left Hannah Moser; 75 left Mrs Y Hitchcock 76 left Tintinhull; 76 right Mr D Burgess; 77 Walda Pairon Giardini; 79 Mr & Mrs Gentis; 81 designer Barry Turner; 83 above Mr D Burgess; 83 below Botanical Garden, New York Bronx; 84 designer Ada Roest; 85 Mr & Mrs van Doorn-Timmers; 86–87 Mr & Mrs Leenaars-Trommelen; 87 right Nursery Overhagen; 88–89 Mr & Mrs ter Kuile-Nijpels; 90 right Mr & Mrs van Eede-Fokker; 91 Mrs H van der Upwich-Koffler;

92 Huizinghe "De Loet;" 94 above left Ineke Greve; 94 above right designer Piet Blanckaert; 94 below Mr L J Ph Groenveld; 95 below right Mr & Mrs Leenaars-Trommelen; 96 Jaap Niewenhuis & Paula Thies; 96–97 designer Anthony Paul; 97 Patricia van Roosmalen; 98 Walda Pairon Giardini; 99 above The Priona Gardens; 99 below Mr & Mrs Gerritsen-Buurman; 100–101 Ineke Greve; 101 above Gardens Mien Ruys; 101 below Mrs M van Bennekom-Scheffer; 104 above Mr & Mrs van Eede-Scheffer; 105 Mr & Mrs Helsen-Buurman; 106 Mr & Mrs Helsen-Buurman; 108 Mr A Roger and Mr N Roger, Dundonnell; 109 Mr A Roger and Mr N Roger, Dundonnell; 110 above Mr L J Ph Groeneveld; 110 below John Brookes, Denmans; 111 Mr & Mrs Eschauzier-van Rood; 112 John Brookes, Denmans; 113 Mr & Mrs Eschauzier-van Rood; 114 Gardens Mien Ruys; 116 Mr & Mrs Langendijk-Egger; 117 The Priona Gardens; 118–119 Mr & Mrs Braam-Holierhoek; 120 Walda Pairon Giardini; 121 below designer Barry Turner; 123 Mr & Mrs Knottenbelt-van der Waal; 125 Maggie Geiger, The Window Box; 127 above Mr & Mrs Langendijk-Egger; 127 below Gardens Mien Ruys; 128 Gardens Mien Ruys; 130 Mr J van den Brink; 130–131 Walda Pairon Giardini; 132 Walda Pairon Giardini; 137 Mr L J Ph Groeneveld; 139 Mr & Mrs Lambooy-Raats; 140–141 Gardens Mien Ruys; 142 Mr & Mrs van Doorn-Timmers; 143 designer Daniel Stewart; 144 Ineke Greve; 146 Mrs L Goossenaerts-Miedema; 147 designer Els Proost; 148 Mr J L Ph Groeneveld; 149 The Priona Gardens; 150 de Rhulenhof Nursery and Gardens; 152 Mrs L Goossenaerts-Miedema; 153 Gardens Mien Ruys; 154 Mr & Mrs van der Upwich-Koffler; 155 The Priona Gardens; 156 right Mrs L Kloeg-Ammerlaan.

AUTHOR'S ACKNOWLEDGMENTS

So many of my fellow gardeners are willing to share their knowledge with such generosity and enthusiasm that it would be difficult to catalog all their names without running to a second volume. They all have my sincere thanks.

I am especially grateful to fellow members of the Britain in Bloom judging team: to Frank Constable and Mark Mattock for their earthy advice on planting containers for sustained results and, especially, to Ashley Stephenson, Bailiff of the Royal Parks, for his advice on composts and feeding, and for his general views on planting in public places.

The Royal Horticultural Society, as ever, has proved to be a bountiful source of information, not only through the uniquely valuable Lindley Library but also through association with the many experts and enthusiasts who make up its membership.

Finally, thanks and apologies to my family who continue to put up with moodiness and tantrums brought on by the need to meet deadlines.